MORE THAN A COP

....

SERGEANT JASON SERY

MORE THAN A COP

SERGEANT JASON SERY

FOUNDATION IV

COPYRIGHT © 2021 JASON SERY

ALL RIGHTS RESERVED

ISBN 978-0-578-88775-3

DEDICATION

To Jennifer, Jack, and Sophie.

You never cease to inspire me and bring me strength.
Every day I thank God for each of you, and none of this
would have been possible without your prayers and
support.

I love you.

CONTENTS

INTRODUCTION

I'm a street cop to my toes. With over 20 years of experience as a police officer, I don't have walls of awards for my accomplishments, nor a specialized degree, but I know and care about people. I also know and care about my job. Throughout this book, I refer to my career as my calling. I believe this wholeheartedly. I've also lived it for most my adult life. But believing it, knowing it, and living it out have taken different forms and challenges during my time on the job. This book is for the men and women who have answered the call to this great and honorable profession as police officers. It's my deep hope that what I have written will be of help when these great men and women face the dark and terrible times. Dark and terrible times that often crush us from within. I'm not a psychologist or counselor, but I do know first- hand how being a police officer can tremendously impact our overall health. I have walked into the depths of depression, suicidal fantasy, and cynicism, all while putting on an outward appearance of positivity, strength, and hope. I've lived moments of complete hypocrisy in my own life, while spending countless hours building trust and helping other officers work through their life struggles. I've listened to them, I've prayed with them, and I've pointed them to resources for help and encouragement, all while living a complete lie. I've lied to myself, and to the ones I deeply love, about the darkness lurking inside of me.

At this point in modern policing, there are tons of resources and research about police wellness and resiliency – written by educated and experienced people. This book isn't about re-inventing resources, nor about coming up with a new and positive spin on things. It is simply about this cop's journey through a job I love along with a family I'm devoted to, and how it nearly cost me everything.

More police officers die each year from suicide than in the line of duty. This has been true for decades, and yet it sometimes seems like it is still just a sideline conversation. Just this week as I have completed this story, I am aware of several police officers who have taken their own lives. It's time to take the conversation about wellness for officers from the back burner. There is help available, but among rank-and-file officers like me, it's seldom discussed. Peer support, physical fitness incentives, on-duty workout time, exist in many agencies, but most of these resources and wellness-related topics sit in silos, with little connection or overlap with everyday life on the job. Newer officers are typically more open to comprehensive topics on wellness, but it doesn't take long before shift-work, daily calls for service, poor food options and life's demands push many into a pattern of talk-versus-doing. A cop's job is complex, and it seems impossible to develop a wellness plan or program that can resonate and connect with all officers.

I regularly read about agencies addressing depression, suicide, and other wellness issues with their officers, and I'm convinced these come from good motives with a desire to help. However, I believe the best way to help is to not complicate things. Simplicity is the key. Complex programs and wellness plans seem to create barriers and muddy the waters. Just talking about these things can bring issues from darkness to light. When cops hear other cops candidly sharing about their own struggles and challenges, its empowering. As I've started to share my own story, I rarely find an officer who hasn't experienced, or isn't currently experiencing, deep struggles.

Within these pages are honest and detailed accounts of strange, exciting, and rewarding aspects of police work, mixed with the deep and dark struggles that accumulate over time. Though I've shared from my perspective as a Christian cop, I believe these simple concepts can be applied to help any officer who is going through a time of darkness. If my story can prevent even one officer from being consumed by the darkness and falling, I am thankful. My heart's hope and desire is that many can relate and be helped. Not by my words alone, but by bringing this topic of police officer depression, suicide, and wellness to light in their own agencies. One agency at a time, one cop at a time, by God's grace.

CHAPTER 1:
THE JOB

The day that I tested for my first police job, my mom died. It's still one of the most emotionally polarizing days of my life. That day, I had tested with hundreds of applicants, and throughout the day I moved on to each new testing phase. I watched as competent and capable people left the testing venue in disappointment. Some I knew personally, and in my mind each had skills and abilities far greater than mine. As I watched them leaving, I felt a pit in my stomach, wondering if I would be cut next. As the day of testing wore on, I found myself still in the mix, and I desperately wanted to let my mom know I had passed the testing and was on to the next phase. I paused while I walked to the high school field for the final physical fitness portion and said a quick prayer. It was August, and the sun was warm and high in the sky.

A few months earlier, my mom had been diagnosed with a Stage 4 cancer. It came as a total shock to our family. She was young and healthy, the same age as I now am as I write this. At that time, there were no viable treatment options, and she made the decision to simply let the horrible disease run its course. By August, she was in her final moments. On that testing day, I left the athletic field at the top of my emotional game. I had passed all the testing andwas moving on. At 21 years old, I was the youngest candidate to pass, and I had somehow beaten out an arena-full of other applicants. I raced home and immediately went into my mom's bedroom. At this point she was unable to speak. She looked like a skeleton, yet she was somehow awake and coherent. She had always been a peacemaker. As I was growing up, she was against any type of violence. I am the oldest of four boys, and she forbade me from having toy weapons of any type. In fact, my first "squirt gun" was in the shape of a dolphin so that it wasn't actually a "gun".

Mom lightened up as the years went by, but she was still very apprehensive about my career choices. When I joined the Marines at 18, she was beside herself. Now, as I was heading toward police work, she didn't know what to make of it. However, as always, she remained loving and supportive. As she lay on a hospice bed, I sat beside her and held her frail hand. Filled with adrenaline and excitement, I recounted how I had passed all the tests and was headed to the next phase. I told her how God had helped me rise above so many other applicants, and that I couldn't wait for what was next. Her mouth turned to a smile and she weakly nodded her head in approval. I kissed her forehead, told her I loved her, and left the room. Just a few short hours later she was gone, into the presence of the King.

Three months later I had passed all the other phases of testing and was offered my first job as a police officer. It was the beginning of a journey beyond my imagination, and one of countless twists and turns. Life is strange and messy, and though I believe that most of people long for consistency and stability, many times life takes us into a pattern of peaks and valleys. Police work is punctuated by these, and as cops we become masters at concealing this roller coaster. We fear failure. We fear weakness. We box up our emotions. We put on brave faces, and we masterfully lie to ourselves about the ugliness we see inside of us. For years I fell into the routine of pushing those feelings down, hoping they would eventually resolve themselves. But this kind of thinking is destructive and rooted in lies.

Heroes

Cops are among my greatest heroes. I've now been a police officer for over two decades, and I have had the privilege to meet and work with some of the most outstanding men and women in this profession from all around the country. I've found that, no matter where officers work, there are certain qualities nearly all of them possess. Most have similar reasons for choosing this profession, which is usually a desire serve and have a job with a bigger purpose than just financial stability. In fact, most officers I've met would say that, when they first started this job, they would have done it for free. I have said the same thing. It's difficult to put into words, an intangible feeling deep inside. Simply put, it's a calling. Shiftwork, weekend work, holiday work – all of it is strangely appealing at the beginning of this career. Like most cops, pay is important to me in a smaller sense, but money is not the driving force. I've always appreciated the blessing of my paycheck and benefits, but financial success has not been my end goal. My drive comes from the next adrenaline rush, the problems to solve, and the uncertainty of the unknown lurking around every corner while I'm on patrol. I've spent most of my career on the street, and I treasure the experiences I've had.

The Greatest Show

Early in my career, I found myself sitting at a table with a background investigator for a police agency I was applying to. The investigator, a retired 30-year veteran of the force, had a street-wise savvy that he'd picked up from years of people-reading. We made small talk at first, and then we began discussing various background related topics. Toward the end of the interview, I recounted how much I had been enjoying my career. As genuinely as I could, I made an attempt to articulate several reasons why I felt this new job was my path forward in my career. The investigator listened in silence with the stone face of a professional poker player. I wondered if I had said something wrong. My mind rummaged through my previous statements, searching for anything that may have been a red flag to him. After what seemed like an eternity of awkward silence, I watched the stone-faced investigator smile.

His eyes peered through bifocals and he finally spoke. "It's a calling. Police work is a calling." he stated matter-of-factly. "I too love this job, and wouldn't ever want to do anything else on earth."

Relieved, I nodded and smiled in agreement. The investigator went on, "The best part is that for over 30 years, I've had a front row seat to the Greatest Show on Earth."

I knew exactly what he was talking about. I had heard this saying before. It's true, police work is an amazing experience which most couldn't fully understand. It takes many hours of walking in our shoes. Clusters of excitement, the bizarre, the impossible and the mundane create a type of Magnum Opus to a show that will fill you with adrenaline, make you laugh till your stomach hurts, bring tears to the eyes of the strongest, and then makes your head shake in disbelief. This job truly is the greatest show on Earth, and I have enjoyed my seat in the front row.

A Different Path

A few years ago, I left the role as a Patrol Sergeant to become a Training Division Sergeant. The move has been rewarding and challenging, but one of the greatest challenges for me is working out of an office. One of the reasons I've loved my job is the fact that I have never been tethered to an office. As I boy, I remember seeing the pattern of people going to work Monday through Friday at offices. I didn't think too much about it, but somehow even then I knew it was not the pattern I wanted for myself. As I grew up, I would mention jobs in the military or as a police officer, and my parents would steer the conversation to some other less dangerous career. I respected their view, but deep down I knew it wasn't the path I wanted. In my new role, I now have a desk, and on it sits a collage of pictures that my family put together for me. It pictures the beginning of my career until now. One of the photos is from my first patrol shift. At 21 years old, I am in in my uniform waiting to start my first night working graveyard shift. The photo shows my dad, my brothers, my father in-law, and a few close friends with their hands on my shoulders, standing in my family's living room. I remember that moment as if it were yesterday. The group is praying for me. Just prior to the photo they had prayed for my shift and the career path ahead. Without question, Almighty God has answered and continues to answer the prayers of these men. I'm thankful for this photo and the memory. It is the cornerstone of my career.

Brand New Cop

During my first months as a new police officer, I was also in the final semester of completing my bachelor's degree. I was in a groove. Daytime hours consisted of attending classes, completing assignments, and sleeping. At night I would put on my uniform and jump into a 10-hour shift with my Phase 1 Field Training Officer. Everything was new and exciting. I was exhausted, but I loved every minute of it. I can still remember laying my head down on the pillow after getting home from a shift. Thoughts of calls and incidents from the past several hours bounced around my head, and as I tried to get a few hours of sleep before my daytime activities, even my sleep felt adrenaline-filled. During that time of newness, I never quite felt "caught up" on rest, but it didn't seem to faze me. I felt unstoppable. I couldn't wait for what the day and night had in store for me. When I arrived at the police academy, I couldn't wait to begin training. I loved the structure, the training topics, and the friendships that quickly formed. I honestly couldn't believe this was my job – that I was getting paid to train at the academy to become a police officer. Growing up, I had never really known anyone who truly loved their job, and I knew there was something special about this opportunity. I remember regularly being asked by family and friends about what I was learning at the academy and on the streets. Within just a few short months, I had endless stories of things I'd seen and learned. I found myself describing my job like an athlete who gets to play their favorite sport for a living. Though it wasn't a sport, there was a sharpness, intensity, and danger that made it feel like every day was game day. Over the next couple of years, it seemed to only get better as I gained experience, developed friendships, and I felt like I was at the tip of the spear protecting and serving the public.

Shifting Perspective

A sergeant posted a great police cartoon on a bulletin board in our locker room several years ago. It showed the outward progression of a police officer's career, and it depicted four caricatures of a police officer.

First is The Rookie, a wide-eyed young officer. Everything is new to him, and each day is full of exciting challenges and experiences.

Second is The Rooster. This cartoon shows a fit and confident cop, with tactical gear and a protein shake in hand – a representation of an officer several years into his career. It's the officer who feels like he or she is at the top of the game, and there is nothing they can't handle or accomplish.

Third is The Old Vet. The officer who is over halfway through the career and has truly seen it all. This picture shows the officer on the phone in a causal conversation. Nothing really seems exciting or urgent.

Fourth is the Old Dog. A grouchy-looking old cop with a cup of coffee in hand. He is at the end of his career, and he spends his days talking about retirement and recalling how things used to be. The years have taken a toll on him.

This is one of my favorite police cartoons, and the detail of the representations accurately capture the career progression in a simple form. However, it only shows an outward appearance.

What it doesn't capture is what is going on inside of each officer. Throughout this book we will look at these different seasons of a police career, and we'll dig into what's going on inside of a cop. More than just the outward appearance of the job.

CHAPTER 2:
ADRENALINE AND MAKING A DIFFERENCE

I read a newspaper article out loud to my wife, Jennifer. I felt a surge of adrenaline as I heard myself reading those words. The memory of the chase the night before was fresh in my mind. My close friend, Scott, and I were working a partner car. We were both hired around the same time, but Scott had couple more years on me as a cop working at another agency. That night, our shift ended at 1:00 a.m. and we were committed to staying out looking for bad guys until the very last minute. Our police chariot that warm Summer night was a smoking-fast Chevy Caprice, and I was driving. It was a large vehicle, but it had an eight-cylinder Corvette engine under the hood. On some of the quiet nights when I was working an outlying district, I would take the Caprice to a lonely road in an industrial or remote area and test the power. It had juice, and it's still the quickest police car I've driven.

As we neared the close of our shift, Scott and I passed a white Chevy Monte Carlo in a residential area going the opposite direction. The windows were tinted, and we couldn't see who was driving, but our "spidey senses" went off and I flipped a u-turn to take a second look at the car.

By this time, the Monte Carlo was already a full block ahead of us, and the driver made an abrupt right turn without properly signaling. We now had probable cause to stop the car.

I've been asked many times in my career what draws my attention to certain cars or people. Often, it's associated with questions about profiling, which usually connotes a negative association with the unlawful act of racial profiling. I've explained many times that the color of person's skin or an individual's ethnicity have never been what I look at. I contend that the vast majority of officers are wired the same way as myself. What we are drawn to is behavior. Sometimes it starts with just a hunch, followed by some suspicious body language that grabs our attention. A nervous glance followed by an abrupt mannerism, an attempt to conceal one's face, a furtive movement – all add together toward what we key in on. Cops become experts at picking up on the slightest mannerisms and body movements of those involved in criminal activities. An officer working the street in a busy area can become incredibly keen at reading criminal behavior in an instant. Obviously, body language or our hunches alone do not authorize us to stop someone. There are numerous laws, policies, and other considerations an officer must take into account before each stop. Establishing probable cause is one of them. Cops are expected to know and apply these factors accurately during every single encounter, and failure to do so can have a variety of consequences. This can result in simply losing a case to being sued and losing our jobs. It's an enormous responsibility with a lot of pressure, as it should be. We are the protectors of our communities, and we are responsible for upholding the laws and rights of citizens.

When the Monte Carlo committed the turn signal violation, I accelerated and quickly caught up as it continued down a side street. Scott radioed to dispatch that we were making a traffic stop, and I reached down and activated our police lights. The Monte Carlo's break lights came on and the car slowed, but it then continued down the street making no indication of pulling over. Suddenly, the driver floored it, and the chase was on.

At the time, high-speed pursuits had few restrictions, and would usually would be monitored at a distance by a sergeant or Watch Commander. My partner began to call out the pursuit while I concentrated on driving. The neighborhood was like a ghost town as we weaved in and out and through the streets and alleyways. I ran through the pursuit "checklist" in my mind, "Traffic conditions, road conditions, safety issues...". A rush of adrenaline surged through me as the car veered left and right through the blocks. This was my first vehicle pursuit when I was the primary pursuer, and it was surreal. Panicked and uncertain, the driver of the car I was chasing signaled turns while he careened around corners, abruptly turning right and left at intersections.

After several loops around one particular block, the Monte Carlo entered a narrow alley and picked up speed. The tires kicked up a large dust cloud, and I could taste the dirt while both cars covered the length of the block in just a few seconds. We exited the alley and jetted across the road to the sloped entrance to the next alley. The Monte Carlo was going fast, and I watched it nearly lose control as it hit the slope and entered the alley. We were close behind, and it was too late when I realized there wasn't time to dump our speed before hitting the entrance. I immediately felt the Caprice's front end leave the ground into the air, and sheer adrenaline and fear flowed as we launched into the alley. I can't explain why, but without noticing, I let out a huge "Yeeee-Hawwwww!" It wouldn't have been so bad, but it came out of my mouth at the same moment that Scott keyed the car's mic to give an update to responding units. My "yeehaw" was broadcast to every listening unit, supervisor, and person with a police scanner. When we hit the dirt in the alley our car fishtailed, and Scott punched me in the right shoulder. "I had the mic keyed!!!" he yelled. We laughed and continued the chase.

After a couple more minutes, the Monte Carlo stopped abruptly in an alley and the suspect fled on foot. A search of the area finally found the man hiding inside a nearby drug house, sandwiched between two mattresses. In addition to possessing an ounce of Methamphetamine, the man also had several warrants for his arrest.

It was an awesome night, spelled out in a small write up in the paper. The article was headlined and read:

Police Find Suspect Between Mattresses After Chase

"A 23 year old man with outstanding felony warrants led officers on a chase through the South Side Monday night before he bailed out of a car and was found hiding between two mattresses in a South Side home."

My first police chase was one I'll never forget, and by most accounts it went by the book. The next shift when I came in to get ready, taped to the center of my locker was a large photo-copied picture of the General Lee car from Dukes of Hazard. I will also never forget that adrenaline rush. The feeling was raw and energizing, and I was hooked.

Teams and Individuals

I love the potential blend of teams and individuals that police work allows. I say "potential" because, like any profession, there are those who push either aspect to one extreme or the other. We all know individuals who are only out for themselves, and we probably know people who try to hide within a team to conceal their personal shortcomings. For me, a solid blend of team and individual accomplishments is extremely rewarding. I've had opportunities to sharpen my own skills, and I've had the honor of working on teams with some of the most talented people I've known.

Both experiences have had profound impact on my personal and career development. Many cops have competitive personalities which can translate into big egos. The desire for individual success and accomplishment mars the ability to clearly see the need for teamwork. I've sometimes tried to slip into the driver seat of accomplishment. When someone makes a great arrest, stops a crime in progress, or their successes are recognized, I am truly happy for them. However, there is always a part inside that wishes it was me. That's my ego talking. We all have one and it constantly needs to be put in check. I agree that healthy competition is a catalyst to great police work, but it can quickly be eroded by our egos. This battle will always be present with no complete "fix", but we can mitigate it by taking a daily assessment of ourselves.

In the movie, *The Count of Monte Cristo* (2002), the two main characters take turns tossing a chess piece back and forth as one or the other has a life victory. The toss is accompanied by the phrase "King of the moment". Life is full of these moments, and we should enjoy successes. However, when being king of the moment becomes our driving force, it adversely affects our identity and gives us a skewed sense of self-worth. It becomes the antithesis of why we got into this job, and it can ultimately lead to narcissistic and self-serving behaviors.

A tool that has helped me to keep this tendency corralled is my police notebook. I open it at the start of every shift, and in the state where I work, we are required to keep our police notebooks for several years. These little notebooks are used each day as much or more than any other police equipment. At the beginning of the shift, officers write down the routine stuff for the day – date, shift, unit number, etc. Then throughout the day notes are added to reference calls, situations, and people. The notebooks are official, and they are subject to subpoena in criminal and civil cases.

Many years ago, I started adding two Scripture verses at the top of my notebook as a reference, in addition to the usual stuff. The first is Philippians 2:3-5: "Don't be selfish; don't try to impress others. Be humble, thinking of others as better than yourselves. Don't look out only for your own interests, but take an interest in others, too. You must have the same attitude that Christ Jesus had." (NLT)

The second is Proverbs 3:5-6: "Trust in the Lord with all your heart; do not depend on your own understanding. Seek his will in all you do, and he will show you which path to take." (NLT)

These have been anchors for me that serve as reminders of what teams and individuals truly mean. I desire to have this attitude and mindset, which brings me to another facet of the job - making a difference.

Making A Difference

"Why do you want to be a police officer?" In one form or another this question has been asked by interview panels across the country for decades. I have had the distinct privilege of working for three agencies in my career, and this question was a part of each interview process. Even now, when I participate in an interview panel for applicants, a form of this question is still a part of the process. There is a consistent answer from those on the receiving end of the question, and the one I've given during my own interviews: "To make a difference."

This answer often expands as applicants talk about their desire to protect and serve. Sure, this answer can wane into a cliche or idealistic talk, but I believe that most people looking to join this profession genuinely have this desire. Those who are called to this job typically have a strong sense of justice and a deep desire to protect people who are vulnerable to evil and suffering.

When I was a young officer, I was deeply impacted by domestic violence calls. Jennifer and I were newly married, and it was beyond my imagination to ever hurt her in any way. Unfortunately, calls involving domestic violence are some of the most unpredictable, emotional, violent, and commoncalls police officers respond to. As a young cop, it infuriated and sickened me to see women and children abused at the hands of a husband or father.

Sadly, there are more times than I can count when I have responded to those calls and have listened to a woman with bruises and a bloody face talk about how things aren't that bad. How her husband or boyfriend is really a nice guy, and just lost his temper. I've seen women stay with men like this until they are murdered. It's tragic and heartbreaking. For me, it's even worse when kids are the victims of abuse. Seeing these little ones hurt by a parent angers me to the core. I've looked into the eyes of kids who are barely holding on. I can see the pain on their faces, even as they smile and tell me everything is fine and that no one has hurt them. I've shaken hands with an evil and abusive mother as she tried to convince me there was some misunderstanding about the report of her evil abusive behaviors. It wasn't until further investigation when it was discovered that one of her sons was extremely malnourished and had a body covered with bruises. When the adolescent boy finally realized we were there to help him, he hugged me so tightly, I didn't think he would ever let go. He was finally safe for the first time in years.

Why do you want to be a police officer? To make a difference. Though the details of how this looks can and will change throughout an officer's career, it still remains at the core of solid cops. There is something eternally satisfying and valuable about protecting and serving those who are vulnerable and in need.

CHAPTER 3:
SWITCHING GEARS

When I was a kid, I loved watching TV re-runs of CHiPs and Tour of Duty. I was intrigued by the portrayal of bravery and roughness of the work. I felt deeply drawn to it. I was also moved by the camaraderie I observed on a police force. There was something about the dialogue, the friendships, the banter, and the closeness among the characters that resonated with me. At that young age, I knew I wanted a career of service. I'm not naive about the influence of Hollywood in those shows, but when I watched the characters going through their "work-day" of fighting battles, catching criminals, and saving lives, I was convinced it was what I wanted to do. When I told my parents that I wanted to be a soldier or a police officer when I grew up, their shocked and somewhat stunned reaction said it all. My mom told me, "People don't really go into those jobs as a profession." It was her desperate and almost laughable way of trying to steer me in a direction she felt was "safer". She wanted to see me in line for a 9-to-5 job. Now that I'm a parent, I can better understand her perspective. However, I wouldn't change my path for a minute. And I couldn't change it, because it's a calling.

Twilight Zone Pickles

One of the most exciting aspects of my job is also something that takes the highest toll on a street cop. I call it switching gears. It's an acute awareness of the uncertainty of every day and every hour on the job. There is something incredibly energizing about not knowing what's around the next corner, what calls are next, or which paths will cross each day. Many shifts are punctuated by bizarre events that not even a fiction writer could invent. Every day is a continuum of shifting and changing, navigating diverse situations, solving one problem after another, switching gears between being proactive and reactive. The physiological effects of jumping from excitement to the mundane and then to the strange can be both draining and hilarious.

On a warm and sunny fall afternoon, my partner and I stopped a woman for a minor traffic violation. When we activated the lights to initiate the stop, the woman turned off the main road and pulled over alongside the curb of a quiet residential street. As we spoke with her, we learned she had a suspended driver's license, no insurance, and countless unpaid tickets for many previous traffic violations. Not the biggest deal in the world, but it warranted another citation, and our agency policy at the time required that her car be towed. With her citation in hand, she left her car and walked to a nearby friend's house. My partner and I patiently waited for the tow truck. About the same time a woman pulled into the driveway of a house across the street, and casually unloaded groceries from the trunk of her car. Within a few minutes the tow truck driver arrived and quickly hooked up the car. Here comes the twilight zone moment. The woman who had just unloaded her groceries came out of her house with a jar of pickles in her hand. My partner and I thought nothing of it at first, until the woman walked over to the tow truck driver. After ten seconds of dialogue, she handed the tow truck driver the jar of pickles. He looked at the pickle jar, and nodded his head. He then turned back toward the car he was towing and tossed the jar through the open driver's window of the car. The toss wasn't an NFL pass, but hard enough to likely break the jar inside the car. Then he climbed into his truck cab without saying another word to the pickle lady and drove away. After watching the truck roll away, she turned and went inside her home. My partner and I looked at each other in disbelief, saying "What was that?!?" We exchanged observations to make sure we had both seen the same thing. We drove away shaking our heads dumbfounded.

Just Getting Milk

Switching gears also includes the public's reactions to police actions. This ranges from "looky-loo's" gawking at a minor fender bender on the side of a road (many of whom end up crashing into the car in front of them), to the scowling citizen recording with their phone while verbalizing that cops can't be trusted, and they will make sure everyone knows what really happened. And then there's the driver who gets disoriented and confused when traffic is re-routed around a crash or incident, causing them massive confusion about how to take another route around the scenario. I've seen people lift up crime scene tape and walk into an active investigation to ask what's going on and, "How long will all this take?" This is annoying and laughable. People's indifference or lack of awareness to danger is astounding and alarming.

This incident happened on a cold and rainy evening when an officer in an adjoining district located a stolen vehicle driving on one of the main thoroughfares. Three young men were inside the stolen car, and when enough officers were in position, an officer attempted to stop the car using a high-risk "felony stop" technique. The driver of the stolen vehicle decided to not stop, prompting a short police pursuit. A few blocks later the driver abruptly abandoned the car in the parking lot of a busy grocery store, and all three men sprinted away. Instead of spreading out in different directions, the three stayed in a tight formation and ran straight inside the supermarket. My partner and I arrived just as the suspects were entering the store, immediately joining several officers in pursuit. Shoppers were startled by the barrage of police activity, and many pointed toward the men's restroom located toward the back of the store. We all took different positions, while one officer gave commands to the men hiding in the bathroom.

One-by-one they came out. As each man exited the restroom, they were instructed to lie on the ground where they were safely taken into custody. When the second suspect came out of the bathroom and laid himself down, a woman in her late 60's came around the corner of a grocery display pushing her shopping cart. I expected her to be startled and quickly turn around. But she was unfazed, and she just glared at us. She pushed her cart within about five feet of the suspect lying prone in the aisle, stepped over the man's legs, nonchalantly making her way to the milk display where she selected a quality gallon of milk. She then walked back to her cart, again stepping over the suspect.

The look on the officer's face who was giving instructions to the suspect was priceless. Disbelief, concern, and annoyance all rolled into one expression. Several officers yelled at the woman to leave, but she didn't even acknowledge them. With the gallon of milk safely placed in her cart, she went on her way down the aisle.

Snakes and Snapping Turtles

Aside from normal service calls, police get called to respond to a gamut of odd problems, notably animal calls. With our eyes rolling, we wonder how a person could think it necessary to call on the police for some matters. On a summer day, I received a call about a large snake scaring people outside a library building. When I arrived at the scene, a few other officers arrived, lured in by curiosity about this interesting call. I'm not afraid of snakes, but this one seemed upset that its sunbathing was interrupted by the police. The serpent was about four feet long, and it was lying next to some shrubs. Numerous by-standers watched with looks of horror on their faces as we made our approach. A couple officers had serious looks, and one burly cop muttered that he wouldn't hesitate to pepper spray the creature should it "attack". As we closed in, I carefully reached down to grab the snake, and it slithered toward the shrubs. Officers surrounded the bushes, and I plotted my course to wrangle it. Several bystanders had their phones out to record the action. I hoped they wouldn't record me getting bit and screaming like a little girl. Fortunately, I grasped the snake Steve Erwin-style and took into custody without losing a finger. People clapped and cheered, breathing sighs of relief. The snake turned out to be indigenous to the area, and it was re-located to a new home near some wetlands.

Another creature that pops onto the grid now and then is the common snapping turtle. I've always been a fan of them for their dinosauric appearance and crazy jaws. These beasts aren't native to the state where I live, but over the years some have made their way here. In the spring, we occasionally get calls when large snapping turtles that have lost their way. Some have traversed into backyards or have gotten stuck in traffic crossing a street. It falls on the police department to find a solution.

When a large snapping turtle found its way into a residential neighborhood, several neighbors had "cornered" it near a sidewalk. When I arrived, I grabbed onto the turtle's long tail, and he immediately stretched out his neck to snap. Thankfully, he wasn't super aggressive and eventually let me pick him up by the shell. He was unbelievably dense and heavy. I placed him into a plastic tote. I then took him to a reptile and amphibian facility, that worked to relocate non-native species. It was a little comic relief from the norm.

Extremes

The call was nothing new. It was a mental health issue. The report was that a naked woman was screaming and trying to throw herself in front of a light-rail commuter train. Sadly, mental health calls have become the bread and butter of police work. It was a hot summer afternoon when the call came out, and within a few minutes I arrived at the location with other officers. We quickly located the woman, just as reported – naked and suicidal. For a few moments we tried to talk to her, but she just screamed and roared at us like an animal. Her movements were erratic and unpredictable, and we knew another train would be by any moment. We couldn't afford to be in struggle with her on or near the tracks, so we made our move to control her as she briefly stepped into a small adjacent parking lot. She was petite in stature, and initially two of us gently took hold of her arms to escort her further away from the tracks. Our goal was to get her medical attention, and hopefully a pathway to help. As soon as we touched her arms, she shrieked and struggled. Her strength was off the charts as she pulled us around. Several other officers moved in, and it took five of us - all fit and strong - to move the woman to the ambulance gurney. Once on the gurney, she convulsed and screamed so powerfully that she bounced and shook the gurney. Her power made it difficult to move her into the waiting ambulance, and the medics sedated her. She continued to scream and struggle, but after a second sedative, she was calm enough to be transported to the hospital.

After a quick debrief with the other involved officers, I returned to my air-conditioned patrol car. I sat for a moment and thought about the woman's incredible strength. I've seen this several times in my career, and each time it is disturbing to see and feel. I then cleared the call and started back out on patrol. As I turned the next corner onto a side street near a group of restaurants and businesses, a family with two young girls was crossing the street. The girl's faces lit up when they saw my police car. The whole family waved at me and the girls yelled "Can we have some stickers?!?" I pulled to the curb and fished out a couple police stickers from my pocket. The family was very grateful. They thanked me for the stickers, and they went on their way. As they left, I realized I probably looked a little strange with my dirty uniform and my sweat-covered face. I thought about the extremes of the job. This family had no idea what had occurred just a few minutes earlier, less than a block away. I'm glad for this. This is part of my job to protect and serve.

I've always loved the extremes of the job, but I now recognize that they are major contributors to many long-term cycles and effects I've experienced as a cop.

The Developing Cycle

About six years into my career, I started feeling the effects of working in a hyper-vigilant state of mind, but I wasn't fully conscious of what was occurring. This is a common development for cops working the streets, as our bodies and minds move into heightened and acute awareness during a shift. I first started feeling the effects when I was working in a neighborhood street crimes unit, and I was having the time of my life. Each day was different and there was a constant flow of bad guys to catch, search warrants to write, surveillance to be conducted, and just plain excitement. The work weeks flew by and, during my days off, I looked forward to going back to work. When I took time off for a vacation or other family activity, I would routinely check in with my partner or other guys on the team to see what was going on. The tempo, challenges, and dangers of the job were exhilarating, and I loved every moment. I was young, and mentally and physically strong. I was working out nearly every day, powerlifting, and constantly trying to push myself further. I felt like I had the world by the tail and I thought I could handle anything. Though I knew there was always someone bigger and stronger, I felt confident I could hold my own in just about any situation. After some of the most dangerous, and even frightening moments, I had moments of reflection, and I realized that things could have gone bad. I knew there were times I could have be seriously injured or even killed.

However, the uncertainty and unpredictability of the situation was like a drug. I thrived in an environment where things were intense and rapidly evolving. The extremes of switching gears began to develop a cycle in me that was taking a consistent and quiet toll. One of the indicators of this cycle of extremes would first show itself in an unlikely thing - Eggo waffles.

CHAPTER 4:
CUMULATIVE EVENTS

The man's body hung from a rope in his garage. His tongue protruded from his pale face, and his eyes bulged out. A boy's Little League hat lay on the ground a few feet away. The man's young son had discovered him when he opened the garage door to tell him about his Little League victory.

"How in the world did this start? How completely self-centered." These were the angry thoughts that went through my head. The house was beautiful. Clean and organized, with custom woodwork and landscaping. All the outward signs of success and a good life. Outward signs. The darkness had consumed this man from inside of him, and now he was gone. His family was now left with unimaginable brokenness and despair. As my partner began to cut the rope to lower the man, I grabbed his body to keep him from swinging. His lifeless body was still warm to the touch – a sickening reminder of how recently he was thinking, breathing, living. The body made a thud as it dropped to the garage floor. I stared at the man's distorted face as he now lay on the cold garage floor. I was so angry. "How does someone get to this point?" I thought and even verbalized to my partner.

It wasn't until a few years later that I began to understand and know first-hand how dark things in my own life can get. Death is ugly. Death is real. Death is always present. I am so thankful to know and trust a God who has conquered death. Without my faith and hope in Him, I know I wouldn't be here today. Events like the one described above are just one of many everyday occurrences for police officers. The wreckage of suicide, murder, abuse, and the plethora of other criminal acts are the day-in and day-out "normal" for cops. We learn to compartmentalize these things. We box them up. We package them in different wrappings, and then move them to places where we hope the memories won't re-surface. However, this is an impossible task. No amount of boxing, repackaging, or shuffling will keep these horrific events from affecting the mind and body.

Pain and Providence

The girl's blonde hair was wispy and bright. Her blue eyes had hope when she saw me. She was six years old. She had a large visible bruise on her face. I gave her a small teddy bear from the trunk of my police car, and I spoke to her grandma while she thought of names for the bear. Earlier, a young officer had been called to check on the girl after an anonymous report of abuse was received by Family Services. The girl's mom was a heroin addict living out of her car with a new abusive boyfriend. The couple had bounced between a couple states committing crimes and avoiding any contact with law enforcement and family services. The report was vague, but it indicated the small girl was being physically abused by the mom's boyfriend.

Reports like this are common, and it is often extremely difficult to track down the people who are involved. Their transient lifestyles, across multiple states and police jurisdictions, easily lend themselves to suspended or closed investigations. Our particular report mentioned that the mother was possibly staying "somewhere" in our city's jurisdiction, and it included a generic vehicle description. I was the shift sergeant, and I worked with the primary officer who was dispatched to the call. He was a new officer, but he was sharp and very concerned for the welfare of the little girl involved. We discussed a plan, and I decided to start looking around at local motels.

It was a busy day, and several additional calls for service had spread the two overlapping shifts thin. The young officer and I divided the city into halves, and we started checking motels and other referenced addresses. Initially it amounted to nothing. As I kept driving around and searching, my mind was heavy with the report of this little girl being abused. These are some of my most hated calls. As a dad, I find it very difficult to separate my own emotions from them. To me, it is unfathomable that someone could abuse a child. While driving from one motel to another, I kept a sharp eye out while praying, "Lord help us find this little girl. Please protect her. Use us to intervene in this situation."

As I mentioned, this was just an anonymous report, and thankfully many times anonymous reports are unfounded. However, the pit in my stomach said this one was different. I slowly turned into another large motel parking lot and surveyed the sea of parked cars. I looped in and out of the parking aisles, scanning each and every car. When I rounded the last corner in the final part of the hotel lot, I saw a car that vaguely matched the description in the call. My intuition said it was the one.

I got out of my cruiser approached the parked car along the passenger side. The car appeared unoccupied, but as I stealthily walked up to it, I could see a woman in the driver's seat. She had the seat reclined as far back as possible and was "sleeping." I sensed that she had seen my patrol car looping through the lot and this was her best effort at playing possum to avoid contact. I peered into the interior of the car before greeting the woman. It was strewn with garbage and the typical remnants of addiction. It stunk. Body odor, urine, fast-food grease, and the ammonia smell of tar heroin swirled in the air. I could see that the woman's arms were bruised with track marks, and my eyes carefully darted from item to item within the car. When my eyes moved to the back of the car, they focused on a pile of debris. Tucked beneath was clothing – girl's clothing. I knew this was the right vehicle.

I greeted the woman and called her out by name. She feigned "waking up" and acted confused about what was going on for a few moments. This is a typical cover-up. I've seen it a million times. Most times, I play along for a bit, but today I wasn't in the mood. I immediately told the woman I knew who she was, and that I needed to make sure her daughter was okay. I appealed to the mother in her, and I spoke to her about the pain and struggle of addiction.

I've used this approach for most of my career. To some, it may seem like manipulation, but that's not my motivation. As a Christian, I care deeply about people. I have a special heart for addicts, and I often talk with them compassionately and directly about their lives. Even though our paths have crossed due to their addiction and criminal activity, it doesn't change the fact that most people are longing for genuine and honest conversation. This conversation was no different, and though I cared about this mother's well-being, my primary concern was for her daughter.

The boyfriend was nowhere to be seen, and I feared the little girl may be somewhere with him. The woman finally admitted who she was, and she gave me her boyfriend's name. I soon learned he was a parolee at-large with a history of domestic abuse and assaultive behavior. The anonymous report was gaining more and more credibility by the minute, but the mom's cooperative behavior suddenly turned. She began to clam up. She started protecting her boyfriend, and she refused to talk further about her daughter.

Sadly, this is classic abuse victim behavior. I reassured the woman that I wasn't looking for her boyfriend, and that I had one goal: to make sure her daughter was safe. She quietly contemplated my words, staring straight ahead. She softly told me she'd left her daughter with a "friend." When pressed, she insisted she couldn't remember the friend's name, or exactly when she had left her daughter.

This dialogue seemed to go on for an eternity, until the woman finally admitted she had left her daughter with her mother a couple days earlier. She claimed she didn't know where her mom was living, but she eventually agreed to call her mom. Surprisingly, her mother answered and she agreed to talk with me. Over the phone she confirmed that the little girl was with her and was safe, and she gave me her address. She told me that, until then, she hadn't seen her granddaughter in quite some time. Before I ended the call, the grandmother told me "Please hurry. I need to talk with you guys in person."

I thanked the mother for helping us, promising her I would check on her daughter. Shortly afterward, I arrived with another officer at the grandmother's home, and we spoke to her and the little girl in person. The grandma confirmed the reports of abuse, and she told me she was scared to call the police due to the boyfriend's violent behavior. She showed me numerous bruises on the girl's arms, legs, and back.

"I have lots of owies," the girl said matter-of-factly.

I nodded and replied tenderly, "I know. I'm so sorry to see them. Where did they come from?"

She responded again in a matter-of-fact tone, "Mama's friend just gets so mad at me, and he hits me, and hits me, and hits me."

I asked the girl if her mom's friend had a name, and she told me his first name. I felt anger swelling inside me, and the dad in me hoped the boyfriend and I could cross paths. I spoke with the girl a few more minutes, and the primary officer and I then came up with a plan of safety for the girl and her grandma. The grandma assured us that her daughter didn't know where she lived, and she agreed to cooperate with detectives and Family Services. As we prepared to leave, the little girl smiled and hugged me. I choked back a wave of tears as I promised we would help keep her safe. After returning home from my shift that night, I went out for a run. I had to decompress my emotions. I would likely never know the outcome of the investigation, nor what would eventually happen to the girl. This isn't unusual. New calls come in every day, and new investigations and new faces become the center stage of my mind and heart. The cumulative effects of these constant heart-rending experiences on the mind and body are substantial.

Evil and Indifference

Fear and distress were in his eyes. He was a gang member, and he lay on the soft grass in the middle of a park on a warm sunny Sunday afternoon. Blood was quickly soaking every thread on his t-shirt. Stab wounds punctured countless places on his torso. Rival gang members had seen the man near the park and had confronted him. As he ran through the park to get away, they caught up and stabbed him violently and incessantly. I knelt down next to him, and I could see that he was conscious, but he was unable to speak. I knew he was dying. I held his hand and prayed for him. His breathing was labored, and within seconds he was gone. I could literally see the life in his eyes fading away. Medical personal arrived moments later, but they were unable to help him.

It was senseless evil, and the scene was surreal. Only a short distance away, kids played on playground equipment and families continued on with their weekend picnics. Several people gathered and gave accounts of what they had seen, but they seemed strangely calm and indifferent, like it was just another day at the park.

The Alley

The clock on my Ford Crown Victoria patrol car glowed. It was quiet, as many early morning hours are. It was also warm outside, and I drove slowly and stealthily through the neighborhoods with the windows down and the headlights off. My head was on a swivel as I looked for any movement or thing that seemed out-of-place. This had become my practice shortly after starting my career. I would quietly patrol the streets and look into all the alleys and nooks and crannies to find criminals. I loved it, and there was rarely a night when I didn't catch a bad guy.

On this particular night, I parked in the shadows of a side street. In front of me was a main road with a convenience store on the corner, and to my right was a long, dark unimproved alley. I sat and scanned the area. All my senses were heightened, and I was acutely aware of my surroundings. A minute or two passed by, and a drop-top Chevy Impala rolled by on the main road and pulled into the convenience store parking lot. The car was full of men wearing gang affiliated clothing. My heart beat a little faster as I watched them. I considered the probability they had a gun with them in the car. They hadn't seen me tucked away in the shadows. One of the men got out and lit a cigarette, while another walked into the store. I assessed every move they made, watching to see if any of them indicated having a weapon or showed other signs of criminal activity. My head was still on a swivel to keep myself from getting tunnel vision.

Scanning to my right and peering down the long alley, I caught a slight movement in the dark shadows about two blocks away. I kept tabs on the men at the convenience store, but I focused my attention on the alley. The movement briefly appeared again, but I couldn't make out what it was. This went on for a couple minutes, until I could see at least two shadowy silhouettes causing the motion. Since it was so dark, and the two people in the alley were far away, I couldn't tell exactly what they were doing. I sensed it was something bad, but now I was in a dilemma. Should I keep watching the men in the car, or should I investigate the two people in the alley? I considered both options for a few seconds, and then decided to go check out the alley. I rolled around the block with my headlights still off, crawling to the other end of the alley where the two people were lurking. The side of the alley opened into a dirty vacant lot which was accessible to my car. I pulled into the lot and drove toward the entrance of the alley. As I closed the distance, I clicked on my headlights and the takedown lights the entire area instantly lit up. I quickly saw that there were actually three people. To this day, what I saw that night disturbs me to the core. One young man had a woman in a chokehold while another was brutally raping her. The woman was trying to scream and struggle, but she had been over-powered by the men. As my lights illuminated the scene, they pushed the woman to the ground and bolted down the alley. They had staged bicycles along a fence, and they quickly fled away on them. I had already radioed that I would be engaging the people in the alley, and at least one cover unit was headed my way. I yelled to the woman that help was on the way, and I pursued the men on their bicycles. I radioed to responding units that I had a sexual assault in progress, and the first police unit immediately went to the aid of the woman.

The men raced through the alley, up through another vacant lot and across a field. I didn't hesitate to drive straight through the field after them. As I gained ground, I threw my car in park and shouted so loudly for the two to stop that I even startled myself. Both men immediately got off their bicycles and laid down prone on the ground. I kept them at gunpoint until cover units arrived and we took them into custody. I later learned that the two men had followed the woman from a local bar as she walked home. They had been waiting for her to get to a secluded area, where they pulled her into the alley and they took turns raping her. It was brutal and terrible, and both ended up going to prison for a very long time.

The Effects

I don't want to give the impression that police officers only deal with terrible incidents. There are plenty of good things that each day brings. Incidents like this may be few and far between for officers in one agency, and fairly routine for others. Many factors such as an agency's size, location, and local demographics contribute to the frequency and ferocity of crimes. However, the fact remains that, no matter where cops work, they will be exposed to terrible things, and a more protracted exposure doesn't diminish the effects on the mind, body, and soul. When a person is exposed to traumatic events, the mind is affected. I will emphasize that though I'm not a psychologist, I have personally and professionally come to understand the reality of this. Many studies have shown how trauma affects people, taking into account variables such as age, circumstances, personality, and the number and types of traumatic incidents. When people are exposed to trauma, the mind finds ways to process it and it moves into many forms of coping.

The same process occurs with police. When we are exposed to traumatic incidents, our mind seeks ways to make sense of it. As cops, this is often very difficult, because many times the senseless trauma we see is ongoing, and it is difficult to apply any sort of logic or reasoning to it. I initially dealt with troubling days through a simple process. Within 12 to 24 hours of "one of those days", I would work out hard. Exercise is a great outlet to wash away the stress and clear the mind, but as we will discuss later, it is a temporary fix for the cumulative effects of the job. I would then move into some cynicism. My thoughts would take a cynical turn, believing that I hadn't helped in the big picture and that there was no way to truly make any difference. My mind would tell me the world is a terrible place, and I would box up my thoughts and emotions and lock them away. This was part of my cycle of pain, which I will talk more about in a later chapter.

This cycle of behavior after exposure to traumatic and evil events is not unique to me. Dr. Kevin Gilmartin describes much of this in his ground-breaking book, *Emotional Survival for Law Enforcement* (2002). Dr. Gilmartin describes in-depth the patterns of behavior police officers move through during their careers. He goes into great detail about the "Hypervigilant Rollercoaster," and the impact it has on the physiology of the mind and body. I remember reading the book shortly after it was first published. At the time, the concepts and material made sense, but I didn't feel the connection. As I mentioned earlier, I felt good. I felt like I could process things in a safe and healthy manner, and I loved my job. I looked forward to going to work each day, and I equated it to playing my favorite sport.

Long-Term

A close friend of mine is an amazing medical doctor, and he is one of the brightest people I know. He has an enormous amount of education and experience, and he is well-deserving of his professional title. As our friendship developed, he would listen perplexed as I described my love for my job. I told him stories and experience that supported my feelings for my work. But love of any kind can dull over time. Most cops eventually move into a cycle or a "routine" to cope with the grinding effects of their job.

As a Christian, I have additional beliefs about how this cycle gets intertwined with my spiritual side. The long-term effects of exposure to trauma, when coupled with the cycle of hyper-vigilance, can have troubling long-term effects for anyone. Dr. Gilmartin and other experts has done expansive research on the various coping mechanisms that cops utilize for managing stress. Significant personal and family struggles are common for police as they move through a long career. Each individual is wired differently, and it's important to realize that the accumulation of events can have varying degrees of impact and take different timelines. I've spoken to new officers who had significant troubles after only a single event. On the other hand, I know officers who are well into their career and doing fine. However, there is compelling research to show that the cumulative effects of traumatic incidents impact people.

The effects aren't always displayed in a predictable manner. One day I was talking to a tough and seasoned cop after some training, and we began to discuss how we deal with the things we see and experience on the job. He described many incidents that had been difficult for him to process and deal with over the years. The officer went on to describe that as time goes on, it wasn't just his memories of the worst events that stirred his emotions. After a long day or week, he would be flipping through channels on the TV and a simple commercial would trigger a memory and he would choke up with emotion. That would open a floodgate of memories and emotions. The cumulative effect of carrying all of that emotional baggage was a heavy weight to bear.

Others cops have recounted how they have gotten choked up during a routine call for service, when something about the particular circumstances brought up a memory or a troubling feeling from a previous event. The last thing a cop wants to do is get derailed with emotions during an uneventful call for service, but the truth is, it happens. This isn't because the officer is unstable, but it's the reality that these experiences do add up and they take a toll. Day after day and year after year, these incidents build and compound in the mind and body. As officers develop strategies for coping and moving through their feelings, unhealthy mechanisms can develop. This could amount to extreme diets and exercise routines or neglecting their own wellness, or by developing addictive behaviors. There are many other negative outward behaviors which are rooted in attempts to cope with and compartmentalize the effects of traumatic incidents. The long-term effects on the wellness and resiliency of cops can be substantial. When not assessed or addressed, there may be a series of wide-ranging struggles. Anxiety, depression, physical health issues, identity crisis, and a variety of other issues can show up over time. During the next several chapters I will share some of my own personal struggles, and how they are rooted in the long-term cumulative effects of police work.

CHAPTER 5:

PARADISE AND DARKNESS

I looked out at the Pacific Ocean from an 8th floor balcony. The morning was beautiful. A few clouds in the sky, a gentle warm breeze, palm trees in the foreground of my view. An island paradise to enjoy, relax, and decompress in. The outside view was completely opposite of what was going on inside of me. I was in one of the darkest moments in my life. For nearly six years I had felt the downward spiral into depression, and I had denied it nearly every single day. No one knew, and I intended to keep it that way. However, with each day that ticked away, the feelings and thoughts became more and more intense. Had you told me 15 or 20 years earlier that I would be in this place, I would have laughed out loud. Though I would never deny that people experienced depression, I believed it was all a matter of perspective, and that most people used the term "depression" as a crutch. It was difficult for me to comprehend, and at that time in my life, it was even more difficult to understand how a Christian could feel like that. In my ignorance, I believed that, if someone was truly focused on God, they wouldn't feel depressed. How stupid and untrue.

As I looked out at the ocean on that awesome morning in paradise, I felt the darkness pouring over me. The heaviness rested on my shoulders in a way that's difficult to articulate. The rest of my family was still asleep, and no doubt they would be ready for a fun and exciting day when they woke.

"You have to keep it together." I told myself. "You can't ruin this trip for them."

I thought of the money we had spent on the vacation, which just added to my dark thoughts. I prayed. I prayed even more. It didn't seem to make any difference. I did the only thing that seemed to help. I went for a run along the beach. The physical exercise helped, releasing endorphins which gave me a temporary reprieve from the overwhelming feelings of depression. At other times days during the trip, I would swim in the ocean, far away from the shoreline. I am a strong swimmer. But way off from shore, I started hoping I would somehow drown so I could get free from my pain. I reasoned that I had a large life insurance policy, and my family had a large support network through our church, private school, and the police department.

"They will be fine without me," I told myself. "They will be even better off than they are now."

Then on one particular swim I decided to do it – just keep swimming. Soon I was a long, long ways from the shore. I hadn't taken a mask, snorkel, fins, or any other gear. When I reached the deep water, I paused to look back at the shoreline. My family was mixed with other beachgoers, who now looked like distant dots on the sand. They had no idea I was hoping the sea would take my life that day. I waved to my daughter, but that wasn't enough to turn me around. I continued my swim and looked down at the ocean floor far beneath me. Since I had no mask or goggles to see through, it was blurry. However, I could see a large dark shadow near the bottom. A wave of fear gripped me as my thoughts turned to what it was. It was moving slowly, but directly underneath my path. Fearing it was a large shark, my mind quickly cleared out of the dark fog, and I immediately turned around and began to swim toward shore. To this day, I have no idea what type of creature it was, but God used it to turn me around. I remember thinking later how incredibly twisted it was that it took a shadowy ocean creature to turn me around.

The Darkness

During that trip, the darkness overtook me more and more each day, and I was hanging by a thread. I called our police chaplain. I told him I was depressed, and he asked some clarifying questions. My ego kicked into overdrive, and I told him everything was manageable, just to keep these dark secrets my own. He prayed for me, and we agreed to meet when I returned home. A few mornings later I was up early again. I sat on the balcony with my coffee, overlooking the clear blue water. My mind felt as dark as night. I prayed for God to help me, and I sensed His presence, but the darkness would not fade. I sat in the chair completely zoned out, almost in a trance, until the solitude was interrupted by my wife sliding and squeaking the screen door open on its track.

Jennifer had known for a while that something was wrong with me, but I had taken extreme measures to hide it. I always had reasons and excuses for my odd behavior, but there was no hiding this. The darkness was physically visible over me. Jennifer asked me what was wrong, and I began to sob. I told her about the darkness of depression and how it had overtaken me through the past several years. We cried together. We were both sad, confused, and desperate to know how to fix this. There was a fleeting moment that I felt better, but the darkness returned quickly.

As we finished the last few days of the trip, I struggled nearly every hour with depression and often fantasized about dying. On the last day, we hung out at a mall near the airport. The darkness started washing over me like waves crashing in the surf. My phone buzzed several times, and I saw that it was a good friend and fellow police officer texting me. I read the texts and it was quickly apparent that he was in the depths of depression as well. However, his was at a crisis point, and I sensed he was suicidal. I pushed my own darkness aside and went into fix-it mode. I called him and we talked for several minutes. My friend assured me that he was fine, and he was just having some struggles that day. I prayed for him, and we ended the call on a light-hearted note with him telling me he was all good. I knew he was lying. I didn't know what else to do, so I called his wife to see if she could check on him. My friend's wife was also concerned and said she would head straight home. When I boarded the plane, I put my phone on airplane mode. A few hours later we landed, and I clicked my phone back on. There was a message from my friend's wife. About an hour after I had talked to him, he had attempted suicide. By God's grace he survived and is alive and well now. After we returned home, I wanted to see him, but I worried that my own darkness would be exposed. I felt like a hypocrite and I decided to just keep pushing the darkness down.

The Emergency Room

In the few weeks after returning from our trip, I threw myself back into my work. The darkness was always present, but I believed I could distract myself with tasks and routines. This didn't work, and soon I knew I was at a breaking point. One afternoon, Jennifer and I sat in our bedroom and I lay on the bed mentally broken. I needed help. I got the name of a psychologist and made a call. I called the chaplain, and also met with a close friend and fellow sergeant named Brick. I started the conversation with each of them by sharing the struggle I was facing, and I told them I couldn't move forward without help. They were incredibly supportive and encouraging, and soon I was at my first counseling appointment. My first appointment was like nothing I had imagined. I was a wreck as I poured out the struggles to the counselor. I tried to articulate all the circumstances surrounding it. I felt embarrassed several times during the session, and even tried to go back to my old ways of soft-selling things and saying everything was okay. I now equate it to being in the emergency room for my mind. Now I was at a crisis point, and I needed immediate help.

This was one of the most vulnerable and dark times in my life, but it was necessary. It was the beginning of my journey to wellness, and I'm incredibly thankful for God's grace and for those who have walked with me through this deep, dark valley.

Since passing that turning point, I've talked with many police officers about the darkness I've described. It's a strange consuming fog that seems to completely take over the mind. It can be debilitating, and it often seems to come out of nowhere. Passing through this journey has also opened my eyes to the causes and cycles that contribute to the darkness. There is significant scientific research into what is occurring in the body during these times, and I also believe that there is a significant connection to the spiritual and emotional parts of us as well. And though this struggle is not unique to police officers, it does have some common threads that are uniquely tied to our job and our particular experiences. Our personalities, our encounters before and during our profession, and many other factors impact our overall and long-term wellness as cops. What I didn't realize when I got to the breaking point, is that much of what I was experiencing was the result of being on the Six Flags version of the "Hypervigilant Rollercoaster" Dr. Gilmartin explained in his book.

CHAPTER 6:

FEAR, BROKENNESS, AND LIES

The dome light of the Prius was on, and a well-dressed man was slightly hunched forward in the driver's seat. I was training a new officer, and we both looked at the man who was oblivious to anything around him. It was early evening, and the lighted interior of the car stood out in the dark parking lot. The new officer drove a wide circle around the man's car. Our police sense was keyed on his behavior. His mannerisms were different than someone simply looking down at their phone. The new officer parked our patrol car, and quietly made his way on foot to gain a closer look. I followed a slight distance behind him. When the new officer looked in the car, he quickly looked back at me and motioned me to come closer. The well-dressed man had a needle in his arm and was shooting heroin into his veins. His addiction was consuming his whole mind and body, and he had no idea that two uniformed police officers were standing right next to him.

After a moment, the young officer knocked on the car window and startled the man. In a hasty and futile attempt, he tried to conceal the evidence. We arrested him after we had talked with him at length. He was well-educated, and after earning a master's degree, he went to work for a reputable company and made a good living. His dark secret was his heroin addiction. The man told us that he started dabbling in some "recreational" drugs during his undergraduate college days, and one thing led to another. In the blink of an eye, with the mounting pressures of life and work, he had fallen deeper and deeper into the consuming hole of addiction. We talked about his life and his choice. We also talked about finding hope. With tears, he recounted that he never would have imagined his life revolving around a needle sticking in his arm in order to feel "normal."

As the man was transported to jail for a quick "book and release," I told him that I would remember to pray for him. His eyes welled up with tears and he thanked me. I still pray for him to this day. Arresting him was not meant to create additional barriers for this man, but to facilitate a pathway to recovery.

There is a misconception about police arresting addicts. Some community members perceive it as an attempt by police to "beef up" arrest stats or somehow fight an endless war on drugs. This is far from my experience and my thinking. My heart breaks for addicts. I have listened to countless stories of addiction. Addicts come from all different backgrounds and walks of life. They are just like me, trying to keep the darkness away. Trying to keep the fears, pain, and hopeless thoughts from overtaking every single moment. They buy into a lie, thinking drugs will help them, and are they drawn in by the initial reprieve. However, nearly every addict I've met tells me how quickly the clutch of addiction brought them unwittingly into unimaginable dark places.

When I decide to arrest an addict, it's because I see that there may be a path to resources and help that they are unable to receive without intervention. It will still be their choice at some level, but if it gives them one more day to live without overdosing and other terrible consequences, then I believe arresting them is the compassionate step to take.

Along these lines, I remember stopping a red pickup truck one day that went through a red light in front of me. When I approached the truck, the man immediately apologized. He provided me with his license, insurance, and registration, and I went back to my patrol car to conduct my routine checks of the information. Before doing any of the checks, I could tell the man was a convict. However, I could see in his eyes that he was clean. His license was valid, and I was informed that he was on probation. I decided to issue the man a warning for the violation, and I re-approached the vehicle. He was grateful, and then he asked me if I remembered him. I didn't. The man told me that a few years earlier I had arrested him. He told me that I had treated him with respect, and I had even told him I would pray for him. On the side of the road, the man shared his story of addiction and recovery. He told me that he had never forgotten how I had treated him and offered to pray for him during his darkest time. He told me he had recently completed all the requirements of his probation, and he had also completed a recovery program through the courts that was run by a judge with an incredible heart for addicts. This man is one of several stories where I have crossed paths with those who have moved out of the darkness.

Though I haven't struggled with drug addiction, I have struggled with the consuming darkness of depression. I, too, know the feeling of brokenness. On many occasions I have lied to myself about the depth of fear, insecurity, and pain I have inside myself. So, I have a heart for addicts.

Fear of Failure

Fear is one of the greatest barriers for officers to admit that they need help. It was for me. Cops are constantly thrust into scenarios where they need to adapt and perform proficiently, and many times throughout a career these can be life and death scenarios. I'm not trying to be dramatic, but it is a reality of this job. However, some of it isn't related to actual police incidents, but due to other pressures in the police culture and the job itself. Pressure to promote, to be selected as a trainer or as an operator on a tactical team, or to be assigned to a specialty unit is always present. Don't misunderstand me, I know that stress and pressure to sharpen our skills and to compete for assignments and advancements has its place. In many ways it can be very healthy. But when the stress, pressure, and competition is all-consuming, rooted in a deep fear of failure, other areas of life suffer and even go off the rails. Again, don't get me wrong. I'm not saying we should embrace and love failing in some twisted way, but I believe it's important to have peace with what failure is.

Failing is a part of this life. We are all human, and we all make mistakes. There are times when things don't go as planned. When we look back, we might wish we would have done things differently. Sometimes these failures come by "surprise," which can be challenging to work through. The key is identifying the contributing factors, learning from the situation, and owning it. Retired Navy Seals Jocko Willink and Leif Babin discus this at length in *Extreme Ownership*. Fear of failure is present throughout a cop's career, but it gets especially crippling and destructive in our discussion of wellness and resiliency. The lie is that asking for help and having honest and open talk about significant personal problems means that you and I have somehow failed. That somehow, we just didn't have the fortitude and grit to get through tough times and move past our issues. That somehow, we are too weak and incapable of doing this, and that we have failed. The truth is that life is complex, messy, and tough.

There will always be people who can move through incredible adversity in ways that defy logic and reasoning. Don't we all wish we had their ability, drive, and formidableness in our own struggles? I would submit that these amazing stories of strength and ability are due to the grace of God. We live in a culture where we constantly compare ourselves to others, and we evaluate our lives against the accomplishments of others. There is endless jockeying for the next rung of recognition and achievement. When we translate this mindset to police work, it is one more burden that adds to the cumulative stress of the job. But when we embrace our failure and our fear, when we learn from it, when we are vulnerable and share it with others, it is empowering. It adds to our story, and instead of becoming the crippling fear that we try to hide at all costs, it brings surprising strength. When we see people at the top of the game of strength and performance, and whose opportunities and paths we wish were ours, we must be okay with it. We may have what seems to be an ordinary life, even within the uniqueness of our job as cops. Our accomplishments may go thanklessly unnoticed, or they may be quickly forgotten. If our lives are consumed by a focus and drive for accomplishment, position, or the next adrenaline-filled event, the fear of failure will consume us as well. This will ultimately leave us empty-handed and hollow on the inside. This is because it is centered around our ego, which we know must be checked regularly.

This isn't saying that we shouldn't have goals, nor that we shouldn't put hard work into accomplishments. It means we need to have a perspective which keeps all these things in the proper place. We need to regularly do a self-inventory to see what our lives are being consumed and driven by. Many times, our drive to achieve is rooted in fear, and fear is a liar.

These Aren't My Pants

He was a tweaker. Thin and in his thirties, he wore dirty blue jeans and a long-sleeved plaid shirt. His eyes were sunken and hollow, surrounded by facial sores and shrouded beneath a brown mullet – all classic signs of a Methamphetamine addict. As he passed by me on his old ten-speed bicycle, the man purposely stared straight ahead to avoid acknowledging my presence. I smiled. I had learned early in my career that those actions were the equivalent of ringing a bell and waving a red flag. It was like saying, "Hello officer, I have something I shouldn't have."

It was nighttime, and since the man's bicycle wasn't equipped with the necessary lights for riding in the dark, I turned my police car around and pulled up behind him. I signaled for him to stop, and he quickly halted his bike and turned to look at me. Behind the façade of forced surprise was fear and guilt. As I greeted him and explained why I had stopped him, he laughed uncomfortably and stumbled for an excuse for riding his bicycle without proper lighting. His nervousness was punctuated with trembling hands when he handed me his identification. I knew he was carrying drugs. While I checked the man's name in the computer system, I asked him if he was carrying any drugs or weapons. "Uh, no." he replied, attempting to act surprised by my question. I responded, "Do you mind if I search you to make sure?"

The man's eyes shifted from side to side, and I could see sweat starting to build on his forehead. "Uh, well, go ahead," he said. "But can you be quick, because I have somewhere to go."

I assured him that I would make haste and not leave him late for his evening outing. I conducted a cursory pat-down for weapons, and then began to check his pockets, starting with his jean's right-front coin pocket. As soon as my fingers passed over the pocket, I could feel something. I slowly reached inside of it, and even with my gloves on I could feel the top of a small plastic baggie. As I retrieved the item the man's whole body began to tremble. As I had suspected, the small baggie contained Methamphetamine. I handcuffed him and radioed dispatch, reporting that I had one in custody. I seated the man in back of my patrol car and read him his Miranda rights. I barley finished asking him if he understood his rights when he blurted, "These aren't my pants!"

"They're not your pants?" I asked.

"No, I borrowed them from a friend so I could ride to the store," he claimed.

"Well, where are your pants?" I asked, trying to maintain the serious tone of our conversation.

With a straight face, he replied "I lost mine, so I just borrow different ones from people each day."

Amused by the comic relief, I decided to continue my questioning. "Well, what's your friend's name who owns these pants?" I asked.

The question hadn't crossed his mind. "Uh....I think it's Mike," he stammered.

"What's Mike's last name, so I can get ahold of him and verify your story?" I responded with all seriousness.

"Oh, I don't know his last name. I don't like to be too much into people's business," he responded matter-of-factly.

"You don't like to be into people's business, but you don't mind wearing their pants, which just happened to have dope in the pocket?" I inquired. By now, even he realized how lame his excuse was. He lowered his head sheepishly, and finally admitted that the pants and the drugs in fact, belonged to him, and soon we were on our way to jail.

This was one of many times a suspect told me the pants they were wearing, which always happened to contain something illegal, didn't belong to them. This excuse is so common across our profession that it has become a running joke with officers I've met from around the country. Each time the lie sounds just as ridiculous as the last time I heard it, but there is a lesson related to all of us. We, too, can easily believe our own lies. We lie to ourselves and to the ones we love, all in an attempt to conceal the ugly sides of our lives. Though some of the lies are as laughable as the man who insisted his pants weren't his, lies are destructive. Lies always lead to bondage and they create barriers that prevent us from moving forward. Our lives must be founded on and secured in truth. The truth will truly set you free.

CHAPTER 7:
TRUTH AND LIES

O n my very first day as a police officer, I heard the word "retirement." Actually, I heard it twice that day. Once during my initial paperwork with Human Resources, and the other time from a sergeant talking with our hiring group. I've learned that, whether it's from HR or cops longingly looking toward the end, the topic is constantly discussed. I'm still amazed when I hear cops, who are only a handful of years into their careers, talking about how and when they will retire. I'm aware that we live in a culture that places comfort and work/life balance at the forefront of life's purpose. I live and work near an area that is blessed with high-income tech industry jobs. It's jokingly dubbed the place where young people come to retire. But I'm not talking about early retirement. The retirement conversations with cops have stayed relatively unchanged since I began my career. It's a consistent, always present topic, and the question is, why?

A Search for Completion

Part of the answer lies within the topics we've unpacked in previous chapters. Like most people, cops are searching for long-term purpose and completion. In police work, the plan and goal of retirement can be a coping mechanism for dealing with the negativity, pain, and terrible things we regularly see and experience. The "carrot" of retirement at the end of our career is the tangible, yet intangible, reward that can help push us through the years. Unlike the job itself, the goal posts of retirement seemingly don't change. It's usually 20 or 25 years of service, with terms to continue longer resting squarely on the desire and control of the individual officer. Having the goal of retirement in the sights can be very helpful as a source of motivation, conversation, and preparation that off-sets some of the regular challenges and grind of the job. However, there is another side that is important to address. The goal of retirement can become a focus that is out of focus. What I mean is that the idea and goal of retirement becomes an all-consuming conversation. It can be used to mask, gloss over, and Band-Aid other things that are accumulating in a person's life. An extreme focus on retirement can cause other struggles or issues to be pushed aside and not dealt with. Sadly, I've watched this happen in the lives of many cops over the years.

Losing Good Years

For some this translates to an officer working endless amounts of over-time, month after month, year after year, with his or her sights set on trying to make just a little (or a lot) more money than the last year. It's an endless craving for just a little bit more. I've listened to officers convincing themselves and others that it's all so necessary. But it also becomes all-consuming. It's an addiction, a drug – the money drug. Our wants versus our needs easily blend into relative terms, and we can be driven toward financial goals with a focus and intensity that is unparalleled in other areas of life. This focus is sometimes developed early, in the beginning years of the career. And though I don't know any cops who decided to go into the profession solely to make money, the steady paycheck and benefits bring plenty of provision and satisfaction. So why does money become the focus? For many cops, it's the means to get to the goal post of retirement along with a sense of completion and time to rest. Unfortunately, with this mentality and focus we lose many good years of life. The drive for career and monetary goals can ultimately rob us of the good life we're after. This pursuit isn't unique to cops, but it does seem to have a unique impact and grip on the men and women in our profession. When we lose perspective on what's important now, we can easily forget about being present in the moment. Soon, good years of life are in the rearview mirror.

The Lie of Peace and Rest

Through the years, I've heard many cops discussing what it will be like for them during retirement. Predictably, most of the conversation is about how much money they will have at their disposal each month, which financial plans or tools they have used over time, and how to strategically draw from different accounts to maximize their income for years to come. Diversified investments, the stock market, and many other things are discussed at length and numbers are crunched to fit different potential scenarios. The conversation then turns to the details and plans for living in their retirement years. Many cops talk longingly about not having to be around people, or they focus their attention on leisurely activities. However, it always boils down to a couple things – a search for peace and rest.

In the state where I live, retired officers are usually issued credentials that recognize them for completing their journey of service in good standing. My particular agency allows retired officers to annually attend a Retiree Range to become qualified for using firearms, which in turn allows the retired officer to carry a concealed firearm. Other citizens must be issued a concealed handgun license to carry a concealed weapon. Each year at the Range I have the privilege of visiting with dozens of retired officers who have walked the road before me. I have the upmost respect for those who have made it to this point. Interestingly, the vast majority of our conversations follow the same threads as it does with my peers. At the surface, the talk is true to form for cops. It's full of smiles, jokes, and stories of the job. I love it. However, as I scan their faces, most of the veterans seem tired and worn out. Many have worked through great pain, injuries, and major personal and professional struggles. Some wear the signs of alcoholism, and others can't hide the significant physical effects of aging after a long career.

My guess is that every one of them was excited to retire and had big plans after the job. They are no different from the cops that are still on the job, discussing, planning, and strategizing for the next stage. Dreams of retirement bring a tangible reprieve from the pressures and weight of their current reality.

During one of the Ranges, after several great conversations, a song by George Strait came to my mind, "The Weight of the Badge." There is truly a great weight to the cop's badge, and those retired officers showed the wear of bearing it for a long, long time. During some deeply personal conversations, I've heard these great former officers telling how the first few years of retirement were good. Their long-awaited plans had come to fruition, and there were some very fun and carefree times. But a change happened about decade after leaving the job. The stories, the accomplishments, the camaraderie, had faded. I've listened intently as these officers described their emptiness and their longing for the job they were once glad to leave. Some fought back tears as their minds flooded over with regrets and the memoirs of the hard things they had faced during their career. Others spoke candidly and negatively about the job and about life in general. This is because of the lie. The lie is that, if you can just make it to retirement, everything will be great. There will finally be peace and rest. But that isn't how life works. Life is messy, clumsy, and fraught with pain and difficulties. There is no utopian peace and rest for the weary, yet our culture tells us that, with enough money and a carefree dream of retirement, we will be complete. This is the lie we so easily buy. Pastor Francis Chan has a great video called "The Rope" which describes how the lie lassoes us. In this short video Chan provides a simple yet vivid picture of the brevity of life. He describes how we pour our lives into a hope and dream of being comfortable in our final years. But sadly, pain, struggles, and death will grab all of us. Meanwhile, intensely focusing on a great retirement plan, fun activities, and the like, will leave us empty and unsatisfied.

Glance Versus Focus

Don't misunderstand me. I'm not saying we shouldn't plan for retirement or look forward to it. I'm personally very thankful to be in a profession that offers benefits and rewards for putting in so many years of service. I've mentioned the extremes – those who constantly look toward and talk about retirement, and those who never even give it a thought. Both are problematic. The key is to a stable future is a mindset of glance verses focus. Glance at the future and plan for it, but don't make it your focus. Focus on what's important now. Focusing on what may or may not happen in the future often leads to long-term disappointment. Life rarely takes the paths we think it will. Focusing on what's happening today, in the moment, often brings real fulfillment, joy, and peace. Glance versus Focus.

What Will A Day Bring?

Like all cops, I've been to countless death scenes. All different kinds of them. Some violent, some peaceful, but death is ever present. Nearly every time, the same words have echoed in my head -- "You never know what a day will bring forth." As I see the lifeless body, I wonder what plans they had in years past, or even in the moments before their life ended on earth. I don't mean to sound insensitive or morbid. Just the opposite. For me, death is always a sobering experience. It reminds me to not waste this short life, and it speaks to my heart of life's uncertainty and fragility. And unlike the evil in this world which holds no value for life, these scenes always tell me a story of its precious value. None of us knows how many days we have.

Years ago, I sat across the table from a mortgage broker who was helping me refinance my house. The man was extremely successful, charismatic, and at the top of his game. We made some small talk as we discussed options for my home. At one point the man said he was getting everything in order for his health and wealth. Intrigued, I asked him why. With a smile he said, "I gotta make it to 100." He was serious. His hope was rooted in the belief that he may live to be 100 years old. My question back was "Then what?" He laughed uncomfortably.

Death is ugly and uncomfortable, but it is a reality. It's a reality we'd prefer to pretend doesn't exist. A few verses in the Bible have hit home to me over the years. "Look here, you who say, 'Today or tomorrow we are going to a certain town and will stay there a year. We will do business there and make a profit.' How do you know what your life will be like tomorrow? Your life is like the morning fog. It's here a little while, then it's gone. What you ought to say is, 'If the Lord wants us to, we will live and do this or that.' Otherwise you are boasting about your own pretentious plans, and all such boasting is evil." James 4:13-16 NLT

Jesus said, "Beware! Guard against every kind of greed. Life is not measured by how much you own."

Then He told them a story: "A rich man had a fertile farm that produced fine crops. He said to himself, 'What should I do? I don't have room for all my crops.' Then he said, 'I know! I'll tear down my barns and build bigger ones. Then I'll have room enough to store all my wheat and other goods. And I'll sit back and say to myself, 'My friend, you have enough stored away for years to come. Now take it easy! Eat, drink, and be merry!'" But God said to him, 'You fool! You will die this very night. Then who will get everything you worked for?' "Yes, a person is a fool to store up earthly wealth but not have a rich relationship with God." Luke 12:15-21 NLT.

And again, Jesus said, "For what shall it profit a man, if he shall gain the whole world, and lose his own soul?" Mark 8:36 KJV

We never know what a day will bring forth, but there is One who does. The retired cops I've met, who actually do experience long-term contentment and fulfillment after retirement, are those who shift their focus away from themselves. They look at retirement from police work as simply a transition into another season of service. It may be vastly different from police work, but their focus is on others, and not themselves. Their faith and hope are in something bigger and greater than retirement.

As a Christian, I believe that God will be my only reliable lifelong source of contentment and fulfillment. Everything else will ultimately let us down, even if we make it to 100.

The Lie of Balance

Most of us use the term balance, and we wishfully talk about our need and desire for it. We hear people saying, "I just need to keep it in balance," or, "We need to balance things a little more." The list goes on. I understand what we mean, because I've said similar things. However, like other lies we've looked at, balance can be a strangely defined and highly unattainable goal, resulting in discouragement and discontent. We can get so focused on "balance" that we never come close to achieving whatever we think it may be. The irony is that we may even become more "unbalanced" than before we started seeking it. The lie of balance has no clear and attainable definition, because life is always in state of adjusting itself.

To be healthy and resilient as cops, we need to regularly take assessment of our lives and see what needs to be adjusted. At one point, it may be our physical wellness. Another time, maybe it's our financial state. It's usually a combination of balls in the air that we're juggling.

The point is, the need for adjustments is often easier to recognize and define than finding balance. What we need to find is a clear path to success and over-all wellness.

CHAPTER 8:
INJURIES, ADDICTION, AND EGGO WAFFLES

In a previous chapter, I mentioned that I started to "feel" the effects of being on the hypervigilant rollercoaster about six years into my career. At the time, I was young, strong, and in an exciting season of my career. The effects and symptoms of hypervigilance were subtle, and so I couldn't connect the dots during my day-to-day operations. I was working a swing-shift schedule, starting at 4PM and ending at 2AM. I loved this schedule for a several reasons – it was busy, I enjoyed staying up late, and I also felt had an eternity of time before my shift started each day. If I got up at a reasonable time, I had time to relax, work out, and do other many other things before work.

Looking back, the first physiological effects of being in the hypervigilant state started to show up after the busiest shifts. I would roll home around 2:30 or 3 in the morning, still high on the adrenaline of the shift I had just worked. Though I was tired and ready to go home, I'd rock out to some good tunes on the way and enjoy a sense of satisfaction and accomplishment from a day of good police work. However, once I got home and walked into the quietness of the house, I'd start to sense a crash happening. We didn't have kids at the time, and Jennifer was fast asleep. Knowing she was getting up in just a few hours for work, I would try to be extra quiet, but this enhanced the loudness of the silence. I distinctly remember feeling my body and mind crashing with fatigue. I would sit down, flip on the TV, and start to zone out. My mind shifted from recalling the excitement of the work to a cycle of re-thinking cases, scenarios, and events. I couldn't shut my mind off. It was on a spin-cycle of thoughts. I'd start to critique tactics and approaches of the previous shift, and then I'd run through potential future scenarios. All good things, but just not at 3 am after a long day.

Many of these "critiques" or "mental debriefs" would involve me taking a very critical eye at myself, which led me into a more discouraging or negative thought process. Like clockwork, as my mind processed the events and my body sat crashed out on the couch, I would feel extreme hunger. Although I enjoy a variety of food, this hunger was pinpointed, and the craving was for one thing - Eggo waffles. I'd force myself up from the couch and retrieve the yellow box from the freezer. A short couple minutes in the toaster, and I was crushing a stack of four waffles slathered in peanut butter and maple syrup. I didn't want a steak. I didn't want a salad, a sandwich, or an omelet. Just frozen waffles.

I made this my routine after every shift. I knew the choice was unhealthy, but I didn't care. I was young and I rationalized that I'd burn it off in about two seconds when I hit the gym the next day. There were times when I decided to forgo my indulgence in waffle paradise. I ate healthier foods, or I simply went to bed hungry. But those were unpleasant nights. I'd toss and turn in bed and, even if I fell asleep, my mind would never shut down. My dreams were strange and disjointed, often involving impossible police situations full of stress and anxiety. Sometimes I couldn't fall asleep until well after my wife was up and gone to work. This caused additional stress. I worried about getting enough rest before jumping into another busy shift. And so the cycle went. It didn't take long to realize that I slept and felt better after my waffle time.

I can now see clearly what was occurring and why. After those busy and exciting shifts, my body had operated in an extreme state of hypervigilance for an extended period of time. It started as I was driving to work, and it held steady until I got home that night. My state of hypervigilance lasted about 12 hours each day.

Dr. Gilmartin explains the effects of this state in his book, *Emotional Survival for Law Enforcement*. Adrenaline flows constantly with several spikes throughout the day. Endorphins are released, and the body's senses are acutely aware of what's going on all around. This is a regular part of being a patrol officer who must function in a daily environment of unpredictability, danger, and uncertainty. As cops, it's also an environment where we thrive and excel, but it also takes an exhausting toll on our mind and body. The effects of living in a state of hypervigilance day after day for prolonged periods of time causes compounding issues. When my mind and body began to crash after returning home from a work shift, my body would recognize the physiology of what was happening, but my mind wasn't completely connecting things. As the adrenaline dissipated and fatigue moved to the foreground, my body longed to return to a stable baseline and simply find rest. Unfortunately, both my mind and my body would keep going until they had to crash somewhere below the baseline. It's similar to the feeling of a sugar or caffeine crash. Most of us know how a sugar or caffeine rush feels, and we also know the crumminess of the crash when it wears off.

Parents can see the rush and the crash in their kids when they eat too many sweets. I remember several times, especially during birthday parties, seeing my daughter Sophie mowing down handfuls of gummy bears and platefuls of cake. This was followed by hyperactivity, crazy amounts of energy, and then the crash. A short time later, if you just looked at her wrong, she'd burst into inconsolable tears.

The same thing happens to police as we move out of the rush of a hypervigilant state and into a crash. Probably without all the tears, if we stay a long time every day in this enhanced state, eventually the body loses its ability to stabilize, and it plummets below the baseline. Failing to recognize or understand this, we can easily fall into patterns of behavior and choices that have long-term adverse effects. Mine started with the waffles. This was my body's temporary fix for moving me from the crash below the baseline to a place of stability. The sugar and carbs brought me back up so that I would feel "normal." This allowed me to rest. The problem is the temporary fix was just that. Temporary. Like other coping behaviors, this actually seems to work for a while, but" waffling" wasn't a healthy or a viable long-term habit.

Military people experience the same kind of struggle. Those who have served in combat and special operation units have described their experiences in the hypervigilant state and have discussed how they have survived the inevitable crash. Most have similar coping mechanisms as cops. But a big difference is that soldiers in combat are exposed to extremes of critical and traumatic incidents in a compacted timeframe. Cops go through numerous and repeated extremes over a protracted period, often for 20 or 30 years.

Coping Through Workouts

I love working out and exercising. Some people grimace at the thought of it. I haven't always enjoyed it myself, but during my later teens, I began to see the benefits of working out and I've since enjoyed the results. I've maintained a disciplined pattern of working out during my entire adult life. Though my routines and exercise philosophies have changed, it's always been a key component of my life. It's been a vital way for me to decompress, blow off steam, and get back to a stable baseline.

When I first started to battle the feelings of depression, I started working out even more. I changed up my routines, and I worked out constantly. When I finished exercising, I always felt better. I felt stable. The release of endorphins would bring me to the "high" that I and craved and helped to push the darkness away. It helped for a while, but then the after-effects of the workout started lasting shorter, and the darkness of depression came back sooner and more intense. The workouts were good, but they weren't a long-term "fix."

Injuries

The struggle got worse when I couldn't work out. Few cops can make it through a career without some type of physical injury. Foot chases, violent physical encounters, being assaulted, shot, and the everyday wear and tear of carrying heavy gear and operating equipment all adds up, resulting in injuries. Sadly, even in death. When an injury occurs, and the ability to cope through a workout is diminished or gone, things quickly get discouraging. The mental and physical effects sometimes seem insurmountable. This can lead to turning to other coping mechanisms that are often negative and destructive. I've known cops who, after being seriously injured, experienced extreme highs and lows. Especially those who are outstanding athletes and have already overcome serious setbacks. When recovering and healing comes along slower than they expected, the frustration level increases. Aging is the ultimate equalizer. Denying this fact of life only prolongs the inevitable. After age 40, the body naturally declines. This is a hard pill to swallow for people who take pride in keeping their bodies fit for optimum performance. Injuries take longer to heal and seem to happen more often. Work-related injuries tend to compound into additional injuries. One injury leads to another, aggravating older injuries.

One of my close friends, also a veteran of more than 20 years, told me he had struggled with many of the issues I have mentioned in this book. Fortunately, he found solid support and counseling and he is now in a good place in his life and marriage. If he hadn't gotten help, two job-related injuries might have taken him out. His injuries were not career-ending, but they were bad enough to throw him off his routine and they aggravated a previous injury. A few years earlier, my friend would have been in a bad spot. The counseling he got helped him to develop some healthy strategies for coping with his setbacks and move forward in recovery. It's hard to act tough when you don't look and feel tough. In police work our physicality is tied to our toughness, our capabilities and our command presence. Some of the smallest, most unassuming officers, who are strong and fit, surprise their peers and criminals with a presence and toughness that rivals giants. Many good cops tether their physical abilities to their police skills. The job is physically demanding at times, and it is important to stay physically fit. Most agency policies require officers to be physically capable of performing the requisite duties. But when an officer's fitness is impaired or lost, their identity suffers, and personal and professional struggles will soon follow.

Body By Depression

When I first began to feel the darkness of depression creeping over me, I felt ashamed and desperate. I convinced myself that I needed to take more measures to hide it. I looked for ways to "tweak" my routines in order to mitigate the effects that depression was having on my life. I felt like I was losing control. I recognized that I needed something to focus on when I wasn't working. But I lacked motivation to do anything apart from working out. Other hobbies I'd previously looked forward to on my days off were of no interest to me anymore. I then decided to start playing with my diet. Not only was it something I could connect to my workouts, but I hoped the change would help my body chemistry deal with the depression. Sinceother things weren't working, I reasoned that acutely adjusting my food intake and nutrients would help. It was also something I could control. During a time when I felt so out-of-control, this was another attempt to bring back the feeling of normal. Over several months, I scrutinized every aspect of my diet. I fine-tuned everything, and I dropped about 40 pounds. I was at between six and eight percent body fat, and the diet and workouts consumed my mind. Physically I looked and often felt great, but deep down I knew this was just another temporary fix.

Don't get me wrong, adjusting our diets and activities to create and maintain and overall health and wellness is great when we are doing it for the right reasons. But the reason behind my fixation was that I didn't deal with the darkness inside of me. And though I desperately hoped that this would be the fix, the darkness returned with a vengeance, and the control I thought I had was quickly shown to be a facade.

Retail Therapy

When I wasn't exercising and dieting, I was desperately looking for more things to focus on, in a desperate attempt to keep the depression away. One activity was retail therapy. I know it may be funny to hear a dude talking about this, but it was one of my go-to activities. I fell into a constant cycle of going to stores and online shopping. Whether it was clothes, books, music, outdoor equipment, or just about any other gadget you can think of, I was regularly browsing Amazon and other online retailers, or scouring store aisles in search of the next purchase. Sometimes it was enough to simply browse and have the ability to purchase an item if I wanted to. Again, this was an attempt to be in control when my inner world was out-of-control. Sometimes I would decide on a purchase, and then I would launch out on a quest for best possible deal. I was still craving that hit of dopamine to stave off the darkness.

Of course, finding good deals and making sound purchases has its place. I still do this, but during that dark time of my life the "retail therapy" just added to my list of temporary fixes for a much bigger problem. I wasn't willing to address the root of my problem. Looking back, I still cringe at how much time and money I wasted. Shopping has its place, but not as a coping mechanism or personal therapy.

Perfectionism and Control

Many cops are perfectionists, and many may even lean toward obsessive/compulsive behaviors. We are problem-solvers. We like to be in-control, and like having the appearance of having things together. We become masterful at concealing our weaknesses behind a tough exterior, even when we're crumbling on the inside. Many of us are Type-A personalities, who don't enjoy admitting we can't handle, control, or solve something. We thrive on bringing stability and control to out-of-control situations.

One year around Christmas time, three of us from our training division were working on some mundane budget and scheduling tasks. We were all looking forward to some time off during the Christmas and New Year holiday season, and we were finishing a few box-checks before the close of the calendar year. As we juggled a few numbers and played with different schedules, we heard several police car sirens kick off when they were leaving the police department. We immediately turned up our police radios and quickly realized that a very violent event was unfolding. What appeared to start as a bank robbery turned into a homicidal maniac murdering and stabbing people at random. The suspect left the bank where he stabbed and carjacked more people in a swath of violence. The three of us immediately put on our vests and gear, and we jumped into a slick-top Dodge Charger. We keenly listened to information and updates being given out by officers and dispatchers as the suspect crossed into different jurisdictions, continuing his crime spree. With hardly a word, we were all on the same page regarding which route to take to intercept and stop this crazed man. I was driving, and we headed onto a freeway, which was the quickest route to where we anticipated this terrible event would finally end. It was the middle of the day, and the freeway was packed. I had the lights and siren on, and I quickly maneuvered around stacks of cars. I felt adrenaline surging through my veins. We discussed our tactical options as we drove, and we adjusted our plans as updates came through on the police radio. A Taylor Swift song played on the car's FM radio, which made it all the more surreal. We suddenly came up "hot" on a group of slow-moving cars. The guy sitting in the passenger seat instinctively stretched out his foot and pressed on an imaginary brake. He was in full uniform but he was wearing his green running shoes. He hadn't had time to snag his boots because we had left the station so quickly. As I smoothly veered around the group of cars and accelerated to our destination, I patted his leg and said, "Sucks not to be in control, doesn't it?" He nodded his head and replied, "Yes, it does."

At the end of this run we found ourselves just outside the mix as the suspect had run out of yard and was confronted by dozens of officers. He wisely gave up and was taken into custody.

After we returned to the police department, we were all feeling the crash of the extreme hypervigilant state we had just experienced. Like all the officers who responded, we knew this violent criminal needed to be stopped, and everyone hoped to be the ones who located and apprehended the suspect. Not for any accolades or recognition, but because that's what feels complete, and being the tip of the spear when it comes to controlling and resolving a dynamic and terrible situation. In our minds we had the perfect plan, which involved us being in control of the drama. But the reality is that control rarely is a reality, and just a whisper can send it spiraling.

Coping Through Alcohol and Pills

When the darkness sets in and we face adversity, it is natural to look for ways to dull the pain. The vast majority of cops I've talked with follow the same patterns of behavior. Many develop the same coping mechanisms – workouts, shopping, etc., but others slip into more destructive behaviors. Alcohol is a part of police culture, and though having a beer after work or a glass of wine with dinner is common, abusing alcohol can quickly become part of the negative coping syndrome. One of my close friends described this pattern in his own life as he navigated his way through years on the job. What started as just a beer or two after work with friends turned into downing six or a dozen while alone at home. Not because of the taste of a cold beer or a craving for the fine taste of a good wine, but to dull the senses. It was to cope with the strange, evil, and disturbing things we take home with us from the job. Alcoholism is common in police work, and thankfully agencies are increasingly recognizing this reality, and they have support in place for officers who are struggling. Even less talked about is the struggle with pills and medication. With injuries comes prescribed pain medications through our doctors.

Though prescribed treatments have their place and role after a serious injury or surgery, they can quickly become a risky way for coping with other underlying issues. Every cop has heard countless stories from addicts, who initially became addicted to pain medication, and then switched to other substances when the doctor quit prescribing the medication. Hardly a day goes by when someone doesn't call the police claiming their car or house was broken into by a crafty criminal, who only stole their pain medication. Cops aren't immune to the same temptations that we arrest criminals for committing. We are just as human as the next person. Many cops have found themselves down a road of addiction that they would never have believed possible for themselves.

CHAPTER 9:

BLIND SPOTS AND BARRIERS TO HELP

Everybody has blind spots – areas where we just can't grasp reality about ourselves or others. Either we can't recognize these blind spots, or we refuse to acknowledge them. This is why we need help from others. When our blind spots are brought to our attention, they can be difficult to accept. Criticism, even when done in a constructive and loving manner can be painful. Our egos don't like it. However, for comprehensive wellness we need trusted people who will speak encouragement and truth to us. We need people who know us well, and who can bring truth and perspective to our lives, even when it's tough to hear. For cops, this can be especially challenging because it seems like we face criticism at every turn. It feels like every "good job" or positive moment quickly transitions into a discussion of what could be improved. And though we need both encouragement and correction, it can take a delicate path with cops.

There are two people in my life who are able to point out my blind spots, yet they can facilitate a discussion in a manner that doesn't cut me off at the knees. They are our department's police chaplain, Jim, and my wife, Jennifer. I'm thankful for both of them, and though both would tell you they aren't perfect at it, they are top-notch in my book. Every one of us needs people in our lives who are courageous and permitted to do this. They bring great insights that help keep us on course, refine us, and improve us, all in a way that leaves us encouraged and blessed. This also helps to keep us from buying into lies.

Looking back, one of the most difficult things for me to recognize was my own hypervigilant cycle and its accompanying behaviors. I've described various cumulative incidents, my feelings, and the coping mechanisms I used, but connecting the dots between the causes and effects didn't occur to me until later when I started counseling. It's still strange to me how we can have an abundance of resources and knowledge instantly at our fingertips, and yet fail to connect the simple dots. Blind spots are called blind spots because we can't see them. Having a solid ability to assess ourselves is important, but self-assessment is still blind to those hidden blind spots. Our ego gets in our way of seeing clearly and it steers us off course. Self-confidence erodes into arrogance. It takes work to accurately see ourselves. Having courageously honest people in our lives to help us recognize the ugly things is crucial for overall wellness. When we recognize habits, ideas, or ways of coping that contribute to a negative cycle behavior, it's imperative that we have a trusted person or persons involved in the full narrative of our lives. Negative and addictive type behaviors for coping must be brought into the light. The more these behaviors are kept in the dark, and the more they are concealed, the more we buy into a false belief that they "aren't that bad," or, "I will get a handle on this soon." These lies only compound and worsen the effects. When a destructive habit takes root in our lives, and it's extremely difficult to take the first step and admit to it and reach out for help in making a needed adjustment. The lie is that the secret is best kept in the dark. When light shines in the darkness, the process for change has begun. It is the beginning of freedom from the things that keep us in bondage.

Barriers To Getting Help

Seeking help isn't easy. The more we need it, the harder it may seem to go after it. As cops, we may understand our need for candid conversations and preventative measures to take so we won't fall into harmful cycles and behaviors, but we can also trip over many barriers in the process. Some barriers seem so massive that taking the first step seems impossible. Individual barriers vary based on factors such as personality, tenure, agency, and life dynamics. I've identified a few that have been difficult for me, and I have learned that they are also common among cops.

Fear Of Consequences

I remember some specific moments when I had clarity about my personal struggles. Those insights were accompanied by strange fluxes of emotions. As I honestly assessed the reality that I was in a bad way and I needed help, I felt great relief. Those fleeting moments gave me a taste of freedom and a speck of courage. I started making plans to reach out for help. But those first steps were countered by a great weight of fear and a pit in my stomach. I would soon abandon any thought of freedom. My courage evaporated, and my strength vanished. I fell right back into the slimy pit of darkness, and the weight of it was even greater than before. Greater to the point that when the moment of clarity came again, I would immediately dismiss my thoughts. The hope was that my struggle would somehow be lessened by not thinking about the potential for freedom. My thinking had gotten twisted.

Much of my fear revolved around the potential consequences I foresaw. I was a seasoned officer and a trainer when the struggle began, and I had become a respected sergeant. My fear was overpowering as I worried about what might happen if I let anyone into my private darkness. I worried that I would be placed on leave, or on desk duty. I worried that I would be demoted, and that my certification as a police officer would be stripped away. This transferred to fretting about providing for my family and how it would affect our future. These were false fears, but the truth is there could be consequences for putting on the light in the darkness. Honesty and vulnerability are always risky. But I've seen that the consequences actually put me on a positive path to wellness.

Attention Seeker

Another barrier for me was a concern that I would be labeled an "attention seeker." Talk of wellness and resiliency, and depression and anxiety, have become common our culture. We regularly hear stories of Hollywood celebrities, athletes, and other influential people talking about their inner struggles. TV commercials try to sell us medication for relieving our anxieties. I worried that if I sought help, I'd be seen as another bandwagon jumper. But it wasn't a bandwagon to me. It was my awful reality. What others thought about me or my motives didn't matter at the end of the day. I knew the truth, and the truth was, I needed help.

Stigma and Embarrassment

It is embarrassing to be a cop and caught in a trap. The stigma surrounding this kind of conversation is daunting. Most police officers carry an air of toughness and resilience. The plain fear of being embarrassed and labeled as "mental" or "crazy" can be paralyzing. Especially for officers who work in smaller agencies. The first step seems to be the biggest – just starting the conversation. It has to start with someone. When police leaders start the conversation, it gives permission for others to start talking. As the conversations spread, real long-term culture change occurs.

Time And Money

Time and money can also be crippling barriers. But finding true help and making real, healthy changes are also investments of time and money that will ultimately pay big dividends. I still shake my head at the things I used to prioritize with my time and money rather than getting onto a path of health and wellness. Even in my darkest hours I would convince myself that the timing still wasn't right to seek help. I reasoned that we didn't have the finances to add another "bill" to pay. This rationale was intertwined with the other barriers I saw, but it also had an ironic twist to it. The truth is, there is no "perfect" time. Life is moving quickly, and the time is now. In fact, many agencies now offer free resources, and those that don't can access national resources, which are specific to first responders.

Agency Barriers

I am blessed to work for an agency that understands the reality and the need for officer wellness and resiliency. I'd like to believe that most agencies across the United States are on board with this, but that's not necessarily true. There are still agencies where the topic of wellness and resiliency is unfamiliar, or not on the priority list. This presents additional barriers for officers, making other barriers seem even more formidable. One reason that some agencies are hesitant to start this conversation is fear. Fear that it may uncover a pile of needs, requiring significant adjustments to budgets, training, and services. There is also an outlying belief that issues of wellness and resiliency are over-exaggerated, and that opening up this conversation would be fabricating a problem that doesn't exist. The counter argument to this view is that the problem is already there. The evidence abounds. No matter what agency they serve, officers will be exposed to significant stress and trauma during their careers, and they must have their agency's support and resources to deal with it. Taking preventative steps and starting conversations will mitigate the potential for long-term difficulties. If we say we truly care about our people, there is no excuse for neglecting their overall wellbeing.

The conversation and resources surrounding wellness and resiliency don't have to be complex. There are complexities among individuals and situations, but some simple things can put in place to start. We will look at these measures in a later chapter. My hope is that, in pursuing these conversations, we will see our barriers crumble, and agencies that aren't up to speed on this will become an anomaly.

Family and friends praying for my first night on patrol.

Our wedding day.

Mom was always a peacemaker.

Montana...

My brother.

Snapping Turtle

Scott and I remain close friends. Our first pursuit together is one I will never forget.

Shooting guns with Jack.

Greg and I had many great years working as partners.

Swearing in as a new sergeant. No one knew the darkness I was in.

Looking out in Hawaii. This is the balcony I later told Jennifer about the depths of my struggles.

I didn't realize the impact of this photo until much later. The area under the rainbow is where God saved me and turned me back. Unbelievable grace.

CHAPTER 10:
WELLNESS CONCEPTS

"Every Day You Don't Work Out, Someone Else Does! Stay Fit".

This slogan was on a poster from the U.S. Marshal Service. It showed a convict lifting weights in prison. It was secured to the wall of the police department weight room, and it served as a motivator. When I first saw the poster, I was a brand-new cop. I was in great shape, and though I wasn't tall, I had a very respectable overall level of fitness. After being in the Marine Corps, I felt I had a solid command presence, and I felt I could hold my own against some of the formidable criminals we regularly encountered.

Shortly into my time of field training, I caught my FTO (Field Training Officer) looking at me with a critical eye. He was a tall, burly officer with a lot of street experience. I tried not to figure out what he was thinking, and it didn't take long for him to fill me in.

"You're going to get your ass kicked," he said matter-of-factly. "You're too small. There are some very violent criminals out there."

He went on to explain that if I wanted to make it through this career, I would need to be mentally and physically tougher than the evil we encountered on the street. My ego took a massive hit. I didn't feel like I was weak mentally or physically, but I started to question this. I was engaged to be married, and the last thing I wanted was to be hurt or killed on the job due to my lack of skill and ability. Being well in this job seemed to center around being bigger, stronger, and tougher than any outside opponent. I quickly shifted my workouts to a powerlifting routine, and I started eating anything and everything under the sun to gain weight. In a short time, I became a large, muscle-bound officer. And though being physically bigger and stronger than my outside opponent had some advantages, the battle with the opponent on the inside would prove to be much more difficult.

A Comprehensive Approach

Longevity and wellness in this career is so much more than just lifting weights or being bigger and stronger than the criminal on the streets. The reality is that youth and physical strength is fleeting. Not to say we can't maintain great physical health and fitness throughout life, but it is on a diminishing path. The key is making sure this area of our wellness and resiliency is kept in perspective. We need to be willing to accept and adjust when age, injuries, and life in general change our physical fitness routines. It is only one part of the conversation, and overall wellness needs to be taken a comprehensively.

Mental Wellness

We've already looked at why it's important to begin and maintain a conversation around mental health wellness for cops. This begins by recognizing the unique challenges of the job, the cumulative effects of incidents, and providing resources for officers as they navigate this career. Chaplains, peer support teams, employee assistance programs, and vetted counseling services for first responders are all a vital part of creating an environment for long-term mental wellness. As agencies continue to recognize mental health needs and develop resources, it's crucial to keep things simple and available. There are many great trends and information is always developing, but simple goals can be lost when agencies strive to be the "leaders" in wellness. The focus must remain on the individuals in need, not shifting to recognition or accolades.

Physical Wellness

The latest, greatest workout or diet will always be around. Every year there is new information on fitness, programs, workouts, and diets. The key is doing something, while remembering that every person is different. We all have different body-types, abilities, and even desires for fitness. I love to work out, but my philosophy has changed dramatically when it comes to fitness. After shifting to a powerlifting model as a young cop, I am now completely on-board with a focus on an overall level of fitness. As I age, I see how important stretching, movement, diet, and consistency is. I can still remain strong and athletic as I get older, but it takes work. This isn't a book about fitness, but as we look at a comprehensive approach to wellness and resiliency for cops, we see that physical health and fitness plays a very active role. Keeping a simple fitness routine and a sound dietary plan, rather than a nitty-gritty detailed program, is easier to maintain. Every cop should evaluate where they are in these areas, but their plan shouldn't be complex. The first step should be simple – just start. Agencies can participate by providing a small workout space, or by creating a basic on-duty fitness program. This can be the jump-off point for long-term physical health and preventative care.

Learning about the value of nutrient-dense foods is also extremely helpful. I love food, especially pizza. I believe that there is a certain amount of joy and comfort that comes from indulging on occasion. However, we know that in our police culture, we can easily fall into the trap of eating terrible food all of the time. The convenience of fast-food and junk-food is an ongoing temptation. Eating right takes work, but it doesn't have to be overly complex. Consistently eating nutrient-rich foods and keeping an eye on the overall calories-in versus calories-out makes a huge difference. Developing a pattern of this in one's own life can have great longterm benefits, no matter your age or season in this career. Yes, it takes some discipline, but the first step to a better diet is simply to start.

Spiritual Wellness

As a Christian, I'm a man of deep faith. It's been an anchor for my soul throughout my entire adult life. I truly believe there is an incredible freedom that comes from knowing that there is more to this life than just myself. Many have looked at the correlation of how faith brings strength through adversity. I'm not telling anyone what to believe, but God has helped me in so many ways throughout my life, and I can't help being grateful. Spiritual health is part of a comprehensive approach to wellness and resiliency. Having a spiritual dimension makes our lives bigger than ourselves.

Social Wellness

As previously mentioned, a cop's social circles often shrink throughout their career. We become comfortable connecting only with those who are in our profession, and often that circle shrinks to just a few fellow cops. There is something special about a group of close, trusted, brothers and sisters. However, we may use that as an excuse for distancing ourselves from others. The gap of isolation grows even wider with the advancement of technology. Now, I'm not a tech-challenged old fogey. It has been the catalyst for some amazing things. But I've seen some detrimental effects it can have on an officer's social well-being. The internet, social media, phones, and other devices can become an escape from the many things we've already discussed. I know, because I too have used it as a way to avoid face-to-face interactions and personal connections. As a self-described extrovert, it's strange for me to even say this. I usually enjoy the personal connections. However, in this profession there are so many conversations and connections that are burdensome and bog us down. An easy escape is to grab my phone and just scroll away. This is not bad in itself, but it has the power to erode our social skills and our capacity for coping with internal issues that need attention. There are times during or after a shift that I want to just veg out and look at the tiny screen. But more often than not, it leaves me feeling unfulfilled. What started as a way to decompress or relax, actually leaves me feeling discouraged, irritated, or down as I read negative news and move through social media feeds.

Change Starts The First Day

Developing a new culture based on a comprehensive approach to wellness and resiliency begins with new officers. Those who are just beginning this career are likely heading toward some of the most unique and significant challenges ever in our profession. Conversations and resources for wellness are needed as much as ever, and the most effective way to begin is to have these resources available at the start of their career. When new officers are provided with clear, candid, and specific information about overall wellness, coupled with individual specific resources, a path of long-term health and resiliency can begin the first day on the job. Having preemptive conversations and resources at the start, before troubles arise and officers are exposed to critical incidents, can make a world of difference. Trauma-informed counselors who work specifically with First Responders are invaluable assets to a police agency. They are some of my finest heroes. It should go without saying that using these resources must be encouraged and accepted. But it can pose some barriers.

Police culture is entrenched in decades of locking down the physical, mental, and emotional tolls the job takes on us. The roughness and bravado of the work pushes cops to maintain a persona, even when it is likely to cost them everything. I love the roughness and uncertainty of the job. I love being in a profession that runs toward extreme danger, battles all types of evil, and brings peace and safety to the communities we serve and love. But the effects and the cost to the mind, heart and body of officers must be talked about. Not just by Chiefs, Sheriffs, Superintendents, and the like, but by cops with boots on the ground. Those who have been and are now in the trenches of the job. Those who leave many shifts numb to the brokenness they see every day. These are the men and women who create change, and who are able to move mountains. With their own testimonies and stories, they bring into the light that which has nearly always been kept in darkness.

When this occurs, culture begins to change. When new officers are exposed to this candid and real culture from the beginning, through the lens of their peers, long-term change can and will occur. I see it happening within my own agency. I've had the privilege of being a part of this change. Now, during the first week of employment, we start the conversation about wellness with new officers. We talk about all the concepts I've mentioned in previous chapters, and we bring officers in to share their own personal stories. Before a new officer goes out on their first shift, they are provided resources to create a path for comprehensive wellness in their own lives. I've seen this working in the lives of new officers. Instead of waiting for traumatic incidents to take their toll, or else letting life's challenges be pushed down and boxed away, officers are talking about things.

Our peer support team and chaplains are extremely busy, but that is GOOD. We must get beyond the mindset that says when cops talk about issues, this is somehow a bad thing. This faulty notion can be attributed to the many issues and barriers we've discussed. It may seem counterintuitive, especially when looking at the agency as a whole. As I mentioned in a previous chapter, there may be a concern that the conversation will open pandora's box and have a crippling effect on the agency. But the opposite actually occurs. I have seen that a busy peer support team, chaplain team, and group of police psychologists are signs of health. It's indicative that the culture of silence surrounding these issues is eroding and shifting. It's a positive and healthy change, and the sooner cops have permission and a place to openly talk about their struggles, the more they will understand comprehensive wellness and resiliency during their entire careers.

Just Talking Helps

Just talking about these things helps. I've met with many officers after they've experienced significant critical incidents, had a personal tragedy, or faced countless other setbacks that life throws at us. Many times, just having a trusted person and a place to speak freely is a huge part of staying healthy. There are some events that have such a deep impact that a cop needs to access all the available resources over an extended period of time to stay on the rails. But I've seen that it doesn't take a major crisis to bring a cop to open up. They just need to talk.

I was teaching a class to several agencies in another city. All those attending were sheriff deputies from offices around the region. I was the only city cop in the room, but we instantly had a connection through our jobs. During a part of the course, I talked about wellness and resiliency, and the need to have a place to talk about these things. One tough and rugged sergeant was skeptical. During our discussion he mentioned that when he has a rough day or goes through personal challenges, he just talks to a buddy. I asked him if that helps, and he nodded and said, "Hell yes."

He was absolutely right. Just having a trusted friend, especially one you share the job with, is extremely helpful in decompressing and unloading difficult experiences. This is without question better than just boxing it up and letting it add to the accumulation of events. Many times, just verbalizing the difficulty and struggle to someone who will listen and offer support and encouragement is a huge win.

Each Life Is Different

However, it's important to remember that everyone is different. One person may be able to quickly move forward after a short and candid conversation with a trusted friend, others may need more resources. People change as they move through life and the job. At one point a person may be in a place where a simple conversation works. However, if they experience several traumatic incidents at work and then face a deep personal struggle, a conversation with a trusted friend may not be enough. Professional counseling may be necessary to establish a path to victory. Regular follow-up from trusted and credible peer support members and/or police chaplains can add to this good path. The point is, though the concepts of wellness can fit everyone, the specific path will be different for each person.

Debriefs Are Awesome

Years ago, many members of my department went through several days of training related to Critical Incident Stress Management (CISM). One large block of the training was related to the process of "diffusing" and conducting emotional debriefs after traumatic incidents. These are often associated with an Officer Involved Shooting (OIS), but the concepts can, and arguably should, be applied to many scenarios outside of an OIS. The process of diffusing occurs within a short time, usually a few hours after an officer is exposed to a traumatic incident. A fatal crash, a child abuse call, a death investigation – these are just a few incidents that fall into this category. During the diffusing, the officer is connected to a member of the peer support team. This is a simple check-in and provides a venue for conversation. An officer may or may not want to talk, but the support is there. Within a day or so the peer support member checks in with the officer again and offers some words of encouragement and support, and provides an overview of available resources. As I mentioned earlier, the members of any peer support program must have credibility. Even if an officer doesn't want to have a lengthy conversation with the peer support member, they are much more apt to listen and look into resources when they trust the person who is offering them.

Emotional debriefs come next. Most of us are familiar with tactical debriefs. We know how helpful they have been over the years for providing honest discussions of things done well and not so well. In my own experience, they have been immensely helpful in improving my response to other incidents. Emotional debriefs have a similar goal of providing a place where honest discussions can take place, but these can have more complex end goals. While tactical debriefs stay in the lanes of tactics, teamwork, and leadership, emotional debriefs dig into more obscure areas. During an emotional debrief, those in attendance include the involved officers, peer support members, and oftentimes chaplains and/or counselors. However, the key is not to have too many people in the mix.

Early in my career I was involved in an emotional debrief for an incident that I was directly involved in. When I arrived at the debrief, I walked into a room FULL of people, most of whom I only had a peripheral relationship. Some I met for the first time at the debrief. It was one of the most troubling and uncomfortable experiences I've ever had. I remember being asked questions about how I was doing, and we even listened to a recording of the police radio traffic from the incident. Even as I write about it, the back of my neck gets hot. It was awkward, embarrassing, and for me a downright terrible experience.

To remain effective, emotional debriefs must be kept as small as possible, with only a few vetted and trusted outside people, such as a counselor. During the debrief, officers are given the opportunity, if they desire, to share their experience and role in the event, and discuss the effects it has had on them. This allows for informal interaction and dialogue during the discussion, but it is also kept on a schedule by the officer leading the debrief. The debrief concludes with information on available resources, words of support and encouragement, and a brief discussion about what an officer can expect in the days or weeks to come. When an emotional debrief is conducted properly, it can be incredibly beneficial, and helpful to offset some of the problems we've discussed throughout this book. I've experienced first-hand how simply having dialogue in these settings has a profound effect. I've watched quiet and reserved officers feeling comfortable enough to openly share their points of view at a depth rarely seen on a daily basis. This in turn starts other conversations, and it is a step in the overall process of resiliency, wellness, and change.

Financial Wellness

In Chapter 7, we discussed the lie of retirement and some of the pitfalls and extremes of this conversation. When we look at comprehensive wellness for cops, it's also important to discuss financial health and wellness. Like many of the things we've discussed, everyone has different life circumstances, and there is no one-size-fits-all. However, the concepts are sound and can fit all lifestyles. Financial problems are a common occurrence for cops, both as individuals and within their personal relationships. The reasons behind them aren't much different than any other person, but they are issues that add to the cumulative effects of the job itself. Having resources for officers from the start of their careers to create a path to wise financial choices is ideal. Providing resources for cops who find themselves in the wake of bad financial decisions is equally important. I'm not talking about some sort of quick fix or a handout, but about help in finding a path to move forward when things on the financial front are crumbling. A funny scene from the hit TV show *The Office* is when Michael Scott admits his financial hardships. Someone recommends that he declare bankruptcy, and then all his problems will go away. Michael is intrigued and eventually shouts into the air, "I declare bankruptcy!"

We all know that's not how things work. But like anyone, cops can fall into traps of poor financial decisions. Having resources at the front of their career can help officers and their families avoid financial pitfalls. Equally important is having resources in place to help when officers find themselves in a tough spot. This is another important piece for creating a pathway to overall wellness.

CHAPTER 11:
RELATIONSHIPS AND FAMILIES

Jennifer and I have been married for 24 years. It's been awesome, but we've also had our share of struggles and challenges. Marriage, relationships, and raising kiddos is indescribably rewarding and challenging, all rolled into one big package. This seems to be true for just about everyone, and we know first-hand how this looks for police officers. The weight of the job has a significant impact on those we are close to and love deeply. For many relationships and families, the impact is negative and can cause crushing blows. Many police marriages end in divorce, and I know several officers who have very challenging relationships with their children. There are many helpful books devoted specifically to helping marriages and families. Jennifer and I have also found a few practical principles that have helped us to navigate through our marriage and raise our kids, while taking on the numerous challenges of my job.

Take Time And Spend Time

Many agencies follow compressed work schedules that provide officers with three, and sometimes four, days off each week. This is great a schedule for helping families stay healthy. Research shows that time away from work and a balanced work/life flow is extremely healthy. Sometimes when people hear about our schedules, they comment, "Must be nice. I wish I had three days off each week."

It's true, the schedule is a blessing. And for those who work compressed schedules, the time away is a needed break. However, there are some other factors to consider. Though cops may have more days off each week than those who work other jobs, many times their days off are interrupted by court appearances, mandatory overtime, or callouts. Routinely officers have schedules with days off in the middle of the week, which increases the likelihood of an interruption. I've heard it said, and I've said it myself to other officers – at the end of your career, you won't wish you had spent more time working and less time with your family or loved ones. As rewarding as the job can be, the time away is absolutely precious, and it is essential for the health of officers and their families. I bought into this early on in my career.

When my kids were young, I would save up all my over-time hours as comp time. For those who not familiar this, when you work overtime, many agencies allow you to take it as pay or comp. Comp is additional time off above and beyond vacation time. I would save this time throughout the year, and when our kids were out of school during the summer months, I would schedule an extra day off every week. This gave me the equivalent of a "mini-vacation" every week, even with work-related interruptions, and it allowed me to have a huge amount of time with Jennifer, Jack, and Sophie.

Taking the time away is one thing, but how you spend that time is another. It doesn't do any good to take the time off simply to isolate and shelter yourself in place. Time alone in peace and quiet is necessary and refreshing, but when you take time away from work, also be intentional about spending a portion with your family, friends, and loved ones. It doesn't have to include extravagant plans or a big vacation. It can simply be time hanging out and enjoying activities that includes everyone and which grows a sense of your presence with and for the family. It creates an inclusive atmosphere where you can positively influence and impact your family. It also creates closer and deeper bonds for the future. When the inevitable difficult times come along, these bonds may help to see you and your family through them.

Consistency And Communication

This may sound cliche, but consistency and communication at work and home is key to healthy family relationships. We all have stories about bosses or co-workers who are incredibly inconsistent in their moods and attitudes. I've struggled with this myself. When someone doesn't know "who" is going to show up from day to day, it causes uncertainty, distrust, resentment, and stress. I've heard officers admit that they act one way at work and another way at home. Others have confessed that their family has no idea what they do, or what kind of person they are at work. On one level I understand this, but it is not a healthy way to think or act. It is off-putting when people act one way around some people, and another way around others. Being two different people – one at work, and another at home – can be a recipe for personal and professional disaster. At some point these "two people" will collide or be torn apart from within. The mind isn't meant to live in a divided state of being. As the Scriptures say, a double-minded man is unstable in all his ways. It's like trying to stand in two canoes – they'll float apart in two separate directions, and the person standing in the two canoes will soon be left swimming.

I also know it's not healthy to share every detail of the job with our loved ones. However, having a consistent and healthy dialogue about our work is key to being authentic and vulnerable. We must allow the people we love and care about to enter our "cop world". We need to remember this to maintain a healthy perspective. We won't have healthy relationships if we don't keep our communication open, consistent, and honest. It is a key to maintaining healthy relationships with those we love.

Take Off The Rose-Colored Glasses

We all need to do this from time to time. We can start believing that the grass is greener here or there, or we can convince ourselves that if we could just get to a certain point or place, things or people will be "perfect." That's when we need to take off the rose-colored glasses. We all have issues, and there will always be struggles. This side of heaven, there is no perfection. I've discovered that timelines, and what I think should fit in parameters that I have created in my own mind, don't often become the reality I expect to see. Since our first wedding anniversary, Jennifer and I have always asked the question, "I wonder what will be different a year from now." Sometimes we've asked this question with a heavy heart, and other times it's with excitement. One thing has remained consistent. Reflecting on the previous year, the details rarely work out exactly as we had expected or planned. We've come to discover that God keeps many of the details to Himself to grow and refine our faith and keep us trusting Him.

Often times this includes simply slowing us down. I am an achiever, and I can get over-zealous about my goals. I tend to push ahead like a bull in a china shop. Proverbs 16:9 has become one of my favorite verses. It says, "The mind of man plans his ways, but the Lord directs his steps." (NASB) These wise words have proven to be true for Jennifer and me. We would never have anticipated or planned the path that our 24 years of marriage has taken us on. But that's the reality of life, and our "plans" are often like dust in the wind. This doesn't mean we don't make plans, but we have learned to be more flexible with our plans. We're constantly making adjustments. This has given us more daily contentment, and it has helped us to keep excitedly asking the question without worrying about a year from now.

No News Is Good News

Early in our marriage, Jennifer sometimes worried when I wasn't home on time. Her thoughts would go to extremes, thinking that something terrible had happened to me. When we talked about this, I remember telling her that no news is good news. I explained that our police family loved us, and if something bad were to happen to me, she and the kids would have a mob of officers surrounding them to bring support and help. When a call for service or an incident keeps me later than normal, and if I can't text or call, no news is good news.

Embrace The Crappy Schedules

During one of my first years on the job, I was at lunch with another young officer. We were working swing-shift, which started late in the afternoon and went into the early morning hours. Both of us also had the middle of the week off as our "weekend." While eating our lunch, I noticed that his face seemed down. When I asked him what was wrong, he relayed a conversation he recently had with one of our supervisors. My young friend was newly married, and he and his wife weren't keen about his current schedule. Though they had known from the start that police work involved shift work and strange days off, the reality had set in, and it had begun to cause some strain in their relationship. Naively, my friend had gone to a supervisor and had requested to have traditional weekends off, so that he and his wife could spend more time together. Then came the hard response. The supervisor simply roared with laughter, patted his shoulder, and said one word: Seniority. My friend was jolted by the stark reality that it could be years before he had enough seniority to get the shift and days off that he wanted.

This harsh reality is a part of the job. It can be very challenging for officers with families to work rotating schedules with inconsistent days off. Holidays, birthdays, recitals, games, and many other family events are missed, or they have to be celebrated on another day off. This is the reality, but Jennifer and I have found that when you embrace the crappy schedules, and purposely find ways to adjust in a positive and healthy way, the harsh realities are much more manageable. We became so accustomed to my days off being in the middle of the week, that when I finally had weekends off, it felt strange. At first, we didn't even like it. It felt abnormal. But strange schedules are part of the job, and embracing them helps to brings peace, health, and stability to other parts of life.

Thick Skin, Simply Answers, And A Smile

Jennifer found that one of the challenges with me working different schedules over the years was the common questions asked by family, friends and sometimes by mere acquaintances. Though I had worked Sunday mornings for a number of years, and couldn't attend church during the "normal" hours, Jennifer was asked nearly every Sunday, "Where's

Jason?" She told me that it often made her annoyed and defensive. A close friend and mentor then told her to give a simple answer, smile, and turn the conversation to something else. Jennifer took this advice, and when she was asked the "Where's Jason?" question, she would simply smile and reply, "Oh, he's working, but I wanted to ask, how have things been with you?" If the person persisted with being nosey, asking her, "Oh, does he work every 'Sunday', 'Holiday', 'You Name the Event'?", Jennifer would simple smile again and say, "Yes, police schedules are crazy, but we make the best of them. And how are you guys doing?"

Having thick skin, putting on a smile, and giving a simple answer is one way to keep conversations from becoming annoying spots that anger us. It can be challenging to do, but it will turn the conversation in a better direction and keep it from clouding the day. Families and relationships will always have challenges. However, we've learned that understanding and implementing the things described in this chapter can reduce stress. This in turn helps bring peace and stability.

CHAPTER 12:
PAIN, PEACE, FORWARD THINKING, AND THE RIDGE

The call initially came in as a dead man slumped on a bench at a transit center. The 911 caller said the man was in his late 20's, he wasn't breathing or moving, and he seemed to have died while waiting for public transportation. My partner and I arrived at the location along with medical personnel, and we were flagged down by our 911 caller who led us to the man. When I saw him, he looked dead to me. He was slumped on the bench with a trail of vomit and saliva oozing from his mouth, showing no signs of life. It quickly became evident that he had overdosed on Fentanyl, and paramedics immediately began to work on the man to determine if any life-saving efforts were possible. Within seconds, one of the paramedics was administering Naloxone, also referred to as Narcan. This drug is used to counter the effects of an opioid overdose, and it works within seconds.

Less than a minute later, our "dead" man's eyes popped open, he began gasping for air, and he tried to jump up. His eyes were wide with panic. He began to cry, clenching his fists, saying, "What are you doing? Let me go!"

It took several minutes to calm him down to a point where he could answer questions clearly. Eventually he was able to explain his circumstances, which included his addiction to Oxycodone. He recalled that, when he couldn't get any more Oxycodone from his doctor, he resorted to stealing Fentanyl patches from the hospital to off-set his addiction. Fentanyl is a synthetic narcotic analgesic, roughly 100 times more potent than Morphine. The man also told me that when he arrived at the transit center, he was feeling depressed, so he decided to "chew" on one of the Fentanyl patches. The "chewing" led to him swallowing the patch, and an overdose quickly ensued.

Thankfully, a passerby noticed something wrong with him and called 911. Had a few more moments passed, he would have died. As the man was loaded into the ambulance, I could see he was hurting. I prayed for him, and then he was quickly transported to the hospital.

This was one of several times I've seen Naloxone administered on the street. On each occasion, I was certain the person was dead, but within seconds they were back. Another time, I was dispatched to a man lying in the middle of a parking lot, wearing only boxer shorts. It was cold and rainy, and the man obviously had been dumped there by "friends" after a heroin overdose. Unfortunately, it's not uncommon for people to panic when another addict overdoses, and they will dump the victim just about anywhere. The fortunate ones get dumped outside of hospital emergency rooms, but they are often left just like this young man. When I approached him, there was no indication of life. The paramedics gave him Naloxone and the man was soon awake and angry. He berated us for taking away his "high," and he shouted that he was going to sue us. He refused to cooperate and give any information about who had dumped him in a parking lot, repeatedly saying he wasn't "a rat." He referred to his fellow addicts as "family." His blind loyalty to them was astounding. Even when faced with the fact he had been left for dead, he wouldn't give us any investigative help. "We all gotta go sometime," was his hardened reply to my questions.

The drug world is cruel and devastating. Like other addictions, it breeds its own lies. It's heartbreaking to see how hardcore drugs destroy people, and how devotedly they will savor every moment of their addiction, even to the point of death. These awful experiences and mind-boggling conversations have shown me how deeply addictions are rooted in significant physical, emotional, and mental pain. Drug use is an attempt to offset the constant and troubling pressures of daily life. It often ends in tragedy.

Pain And Peace

When I finally took the steps to get into counseling, it was life changing. My counselor connected dots in my story that I couldn't have done without his insights. During several sessions, he walked me through a psychological path that his mentor, Dr. Terry

Hargrave, had created and developed. My counselor described it as "brilliantly simple," and I couldn't agree more. It involves something referred to as the Pain Cycle and Peace Cycle, and the process has become unbelievably helpful in my life. For me, the process is based around my faith as a Christian, but it is also tied to how the brain functions, specifically through neuroplasticity. I don't have comprehensive understanding of how the brain works, but I do have a general understanding of how this works. Neuroplasticity is the brain's "plasticity." It refers to the ability of the brain's neural networks or pathways to change and reorganize. Neuroscientists have discovered that changes which were once believed to occur only during childhood brain development actually continue into adulthood. This discovery has many awesome implications. It means scientists now understand that our brain has the ability to heal itself, even after exposure to trauma later in life.

Obviously, the process has a specific path that is unique to each individual. This knowledge applied to my own specific journey has had a tremendous effect on my healing process and resiliency. Each of us has had painful experiences. Some pain is related to our own choices, and some is a result of the world we live in. We all have a unique story, and whether we have been exposed to much pain or little, our brain develops ways to deal or cope with it.

For me, it started when I was a young boy. During pain or stress, my brain found ways to manage it, but it often rolled into unhealthy thinking, poor choices and bad behaviors. My brain developed a mental process that flowed through my neural networks thousands of times, year after year, creating paths that became an instant "go-to" during stress. When feelings of insecurity, unworthiness, and shame crept in, my mind immediately went into a cycle of pain. Then I would typically fall into some type of negative coping behavior. The ways I coped changed somewhat over the years, but eventually this pain cycle took its toll to the extreme, and I found myself despondently swimming off the shores of Hawaii.

This Pain Cycle can be applied to anyone. It even applies on a larger scale to communities, and even to a whole society. Pain and adversity are a part of this world. As a Christian, I believe it will continue until all of God's promises have been fulfilled. But in the meantime, we have to consider how to navigate through the diverse challenges that life throws at us, even when those difficulties are a result of our own choices. As cops, we have many similar and shared traumatic experiences from the job that affect our cycle of pain. The cycles we developed when we were young will continue and expand as we get further into this job. When we are triggered through stressful events, our pain cycle starts up again. The coping may take different forms over time, but it usually leads to destructive behaviors as we head further down the road. This is the Pain Cycle. Although our brain has been down the pain cycle path thousands of times before, it is still able to retrain itself. This is the process that Dr. Hargrave calls the Peace Cycle. It begins by looking into our individual story and identifying our distinctive cycles of pain. It also takes into account our personalities, our various experiences, and many other aspects of our unique makeup. This includes watching for specific trigger points and their associated emotional reactions. This is not a one-size-fits-all therapeutic model. There is a variety of helpful approaches to counseling and therapy. I've found this concept tremendously helpful to me. With the aid of my counselor, I've worked through many besetting issues that are specific to my story, and I've experienced the personal freedom that comes from entering into a cycle of peace. Over time and a journey which continues to this day, I've learned how to retrain my brain to deal with trigger events in a healthy and productive manner. For me, it's been brilliantly simple.

When The Darkness Sets In

One important thing to understand when discussing the pain and peace cycles of our own story is that there is no perfect "fix." I have come to recognize that there will never be a time in this life where I am completely free from all insecurity, shame, or depression. For me, the key is understanding what these feelings and emotions are rooted in and how they are triggered. With this knowledge and understanding, I can move forward. I'm now equipped with tools to help me manage my stress and problems more effectively. The negative stuff doesn't have such a powerful grip on me as before. When the darkness sets in, and I can feel to my very core that it's going to be a day of battle, I have a totally new approach to dealing with it. I recognize that it's okay for me to have these feelings and emotions. Instead of trying to push them aside or box them up, I have learned to accept them and work through them. This seems counter-intuitive, especially in a culture that tries to avoid pain and discomfort at all costs. This has been true of me. I've tried stuffing my emotions inside myself and putting a lid on them, blindly believing that they would somehow be closed up forever with no more lingering pain.

Although some parts of my story are truly specific and unique to me, I've discovered that I am not alone in this struggle. There are similar paths and feelings that we all share. We've all had days when the darkness seems to creep over us. For me, it starts as a small pit in my stomach. I've learned to sense it even when it seems to still be a million miles away. It's like the feeling I get after staying up all night working a graveyard shift. It's a crawling sensation of tiredness, mixed with a weird feeling of growing hunger. On days or moments when this feeling starts to build, I immediately move into proactively managing it. This means simply embracing it for what it is, and getting a grip on it before it gets a grip on me. I am aware of when I am most susceptible to these unwelcome intrusions. Between 3 and 5 pm, when I'm not actively working, working out, or busy with some task, I can feel the familiar darkness coming over me. It's been this way for as long as I can remember. I don't know if there is a person on this planet that could figure it out. It may be related to my body's rhythm, something rooted in my childhood, or something way outside my reach. But the point is to know that when it happens, there are healthy ways to manage it. None of us is alone in this.

Forward Thinking

"No regrets." We've all heard this phrase. When people say they have no regrets, I wonder if it's a way of trying to convince themselves that their regrets don't exist. For me, the truth is that my regrets are real. I regret some things I've said and done. I honestly regret not reaching out for help sooner than I did. But I'm also incredibly thankful for God's grace and protection. His timing is perfect, even if I didn't seek help as soon as I should have. Knowing this helps to keep me from dwelling on my regrets. My triggers will never go away. My pain cycles and peace cycles will always be a part of life on earth, and it saddens me that so many people move through life without finding help and freedom. Thankfully, I have a faith that anchors me despite my weaknesses and the uncertainties that I face every day.

Adversity is often rooted in our own decisions, even choices we made long ago. Some choices and consequences can shackle us for a lifetime and may seem impossible to break free from. Our thoughts and feelings seem to conspire in agreement with these nagging memories of failure and regret. Some thoughts become so intrusive, they create significant barriers to getting through the moment, or the day, or even longer. This is why it is important to understand how to move out of the past and into a progressive mode of thinking – forward thinking. Training our brains toward developing a peace cycle means just glancing at regrets like traffic in a rearview mirror, but not dwelling on them. Driving down the road with our eyes riveted on what's behind us would result in a crash. In the same way, it's vital to keep thinking forward.

A favorite Bible verse of mine is found in the Book of Lamentations, which is a book about sadness, hence its title. But despite the sad reality that it depicts, in Chapter 3 the author insists that God's "mercies are new every morning" (Lam. 3:22-24). My heart rests daily in this promise, and so I am encouraged to go into my day thinking forward. When I was a kid my mom used to sing a pithy song called "Count Your Blessings." There are times, however, when perhaps the only blessing we can see to count is that we are still alive and breathing. But even counting this basic reality can help shift our perspective from the downside of our circumstances. It helps to move our minds forward. It seems simple, but simple isn't always easy.

The Ridge

There are moments in life that are distinctly and unforgettably life changing. One of these moments happened when I was standing atop a high volcanic ridge on the slopes of Mount Hood. On a cold sunny day, my family had hiked into a place called White River Canyon to go sledding. It's one of our favorite places to sled. During the hike, air was incredibly clean and refreshing. As it filled my lungs, I felt completely at peace. Eventually, I took a break from sledding and made my way high up to the ridge that overlooked the canyon. I could see my family in the distance, sledding and enjoying the beauty of the creation. The breeze was cold, but not uncomfortable. The sun felt warm despite the wintry air. In that brief moment, I realized that I was breathing much more than clean mountain air. I was breathing in God's love and forgiveness and grace. My mind and heart felt deeply cleansed and refreshed. It was one of the greatest moments in my healing. It was a simple, clear, defining moment that I can consciously remember whenever the pain cycle comes back over me. When I feel myself slipping backwards from forward thinking, my mind goes back to that ridge and I think about the clarity and peace I experienced in that single moment. It reminds me to count my blessings. It helps me to focus on God's grace, and it prompts me to keep thinking forward. I hope you have a place like The Ridge that comes to your mind when adversity strikes you and the darkness tries to hijack your thinking. When that happens, I encourage you to pause for a few moments and recall a place of peace that you've experienced. A simple breath of fresh air from that place can do wonders for your perspective.

It's like taking a hike to your personal "happy place," for a very important purpose. The Ridge is my place. It's a constant reminder that I am still climbing the path to wellness.

CHAPTER 13:
ADVERSITY

A bout a third of the way through my career, I was involved in a deadly use of force. It happened late on a Sunday afternoon in the Spring. No one could have prepared me and my family for the aftermath, and I'm thankful Jennifer and Jack were out of town visiting her parents in Montana. Sophie wasn't yet born. The day started routinely, but like all shifts in this profession, it became a stark reminder that we never know what a day may bring forth.

My usual partner had arrived to work early for some extra duty, and wasn't scheduled to join me until later in the shift. My initial plan was to simply hang at the station and catch up on paperwork, but a friend working a solo car invited me to jump in with him until my partner returned. Going out on the road sounded much better than paperwork, so I didn't hesitate to take him up on the invitation.

An hour into the shift, a car caught my partner's attention as we patrolled down a residential street. At first, I missed it since I was completing a task on our patrol car's computer. We looped around the block and located the car traveling on a main road. My partner quickly caught up and initiated a traffic stop for violations the driver had committed. There were quite a few unknowns, which is usually the case during traffic stops. I didn't realize the driver had a passenger when my partner first saw the car, but now the passenger was gone. I also didn't know until later that the driver had high levels of cocaine in his system, nor that he had nearly an ounce of packaged crack cocaine concealed in his mouth. These and many other details also came to light after the incident.

Shortly after the stop, the circumstances changed in a matter of seconds. The man was uncooperative from the start. But then he began reaching around the car and into his pockets. Every bit of his behavior and movements indicated he was retrieving a weapon, and moments later I fired my pistol, hitting the man three times.

In the brief moments leading up to the shots, I had a clarity like something I had never experienced. I felt calm and clear. All of my senses were at a level of unbelievable acuity. But it was not a situation that I ever wanted to be in. I've never met a cop who hopes to use deadly force. We are trained and willing, as we protect and serve our communities, but we hope to avoid using force when possible.

After the shooting, my adrenaline caught up with me. My partner and I moved back to our patrol car. I radioed in additional units and medical personnel, and soon other officers arrived and approached the man's car. Since I was the involved officer, I stood off at distance near a group of police cars. More people arrived, including command staff and a police association attorney. I sat down inside a police car with the attorney and started to go through the details of the shooting. My hands trembled as my body processed all the psychological and physiological effects of this event. Then I learned that the man was dead.

As I conversed with the attorney, providing details of the incident, my mind was racing. Through the police car windshield, I watched as a crowd of people grew around the scene. Angry faces surrounded the perimeter of the crime scene tape. Officers tried to keep people calm, but the crowd grew more and more hostile. Waves of helplessness, uncertainty, and fear washed over me. Details seemed strangely hidden from me as I watched officers and investigators speak with each other. Their somber faces and quick glances in my direction told me I was missing something. I felt a pit in my stomach grow as I racked my mind trying to figure out what all the discussions were about. As the situation grew more intense, the attorney came back to the car with news. His eyes were serious and intense. He paused for a moment and said "Jason, they didn't find a gun."

My heart sank. "What?!" I asked in confusion. I again described all the things leading up to the incident. In my mind, there was no question the man had a gun. A few moments later I was driven from the scene back to the precinct. This was also the last time I would be able to see or speak with my partner for quite some time. As the next hours unfolded, I had cops all around me offering words of encouragement and support. But I felt incredibly alone. I prayed. My mind was on overdrive as I recounted details of the incident, trying to piece it all together. Detectives met with me and took all my clothing and gear, which included my gun and badge. This is standard procedure after any shooting, as it is all considered evidence, but it still felt strangely awful.

The process continued late into the evening, until I was finally able to head home. My younger brother was in the loop with what had happened, and he offered to have me stay at his apartment for the night. Though I just wanted to go home, I knew it was the right thing to do. I was actually glad to have his company. As I settled onto the couch at his place, I felt mentally and physically exhausted. I still felt out of the loop on the full details, and I had trouble shutting down my racing mind. My brother clicked on the TV to the local news, and the shooting was a top story on every channel. Most of it was based on speculation and non-eyewitness testimony. It was difficult to watch. We eventually shut it off, and I felt deeply discouraged as I laid my head down on the pillow. I prayed and poured out my heart to God as I drifted off to sleep. The next morning, I woke up early, and I briefly spoke with my brother before he headed off to work. I gathered my things and finally drove home. Seconds after I had left my brother's apartment, while driving onto a main road, a motorcycle cop from a neighboring agency pulled up next to me. I recognized him, and we turned onto a side street. News travels fast, and he had already heard a few details about the shooting incident. We spoke briefly, and he offered words of support and encouragement before we parted ways.

When I arrived home, I still felt exhausted. I knew there would be an enormous volume of calls and conversations throughout the day, and I sat on the couch in silence. I thanked God for the day, and I opened my Bible to where I left off reading the day before. Taking out the bookmark, I opened it to where I had stopped reading at Psalm 139. I began to read. The words quickly became another defining moment in my life. I felt peace. I knew God was with me and in control, and that He would carry me through this. But I had no idea how difficult the next couple months would be.

Aftermath

The next few weeks became a whirlwind of phone calls, meetings, and media attention. My partner and I were assigned defense attorneys, and interviews were scheduled with detectives, internal affairs investigators, members of the police association, and the district attorney's office. Each day felt heavy and full, and there wasn't even a remote end in sight. The media was in a relentless frenzy, searching to find out everything about me and my family. It was by no means an attempt to find the truth.

Jennifer and Jack remained in Montana as the aftermath of it all increased daily. One day I was preparing for another meeting when Jennifer called me and exclaimed, "There's a reporter at your dad's house right now!" There was an urgency and anger in her voice. That day Jennifer had decided to swing by my dad's house, which wasn't far from where her parents lived. When she walked up to the house, she discovered that my dad was comfortably settled in and talking to a reporter from the Portland area. Jennifer quickly ushered the man out of the house, and as politely as possible, given the circumstances, she asked my dad not to talk to anyone else about me or our family. He had been duped into thinking that he was simply bringing some positive truth into the mix, but the motives on the other side were far from honorable. I later found out that members of the media had even gone to my high school to interview former teachers. Several anti-police groups also started making threats toward me and my family. Wanted posters with my picture showed up in different parts of the city, and our home address and phone number were posted on different websites. It was surreal, and each day felt more and more terrible and uncertain.

When Jennifer and Jack returned home, it was a nice reprieve from the daily grind. Due to the threats and volatility of the situation, the police department put a panic alarm in our house. I could see the stress on Jennifer's face, but our deep faith pulled us through each day. The coming days and weeks had an oddly mixed feeling of just dragging along and yet flying by. The level of support was also off the charts. Each day I was flooded with calls, emails, and cards of support and encouragement. Friends and pastoral staff from our church were constantly present for support, as were countless police officers.

I say officers because, sadly, very few above the rank of sergeant contacted me outside of official business. Being further down the road now, I have a better understanding of the pressures and politics in the upper ranks of command. Though I sensed there was support, the outward expression of it wasn't there. There were a few in the higher ranks that did contact me. To this day they rank among the most successful leaders in the police world.

On one particularly tough day, an officer stopped by the house. He later moved up the ranks to become second-in-command of the agency. He simply wanted to check in and offer some encouragement and support. He took a minute to pray with me. It was exactly what I needed that day, and he was one of many who God brought in at the perfect time. At the time we also didn't live in the city where I worked. However, the law enforcement community is close-knit and unbelievably supportive. Routinely, I would look out my window at night and see deputies parked outside our home. It was a tremendous blessing to our family, and we all slept better knowing they were keeping watch.

The Inquest

I can still vividly remember the conversation with my attorney. He told me that the city and agency were going to conduct a public inquest. This was to provide transparency and to answer questions by a very vocal segment of the community. He told me the inquest would be intense, and media would be present in droves. He also discussed ways we could block my participating in this event by filing a lawsuit. I felt sick just thinking about it.

Over the next couple days Jennifer and I looked at how this could affect our lives, and we asked people close to us for prayer. I made the decision to participate, and I quickly gained an understanding of what the inquest entails. I learned that the inquest had six jurors with a limited scope and role. The entire event didn't have any actual bearing like a criminal or civil proceeding, but it would be held at the main courthouse, and it would be open to an audience of police, citizens, and media. On the morning of the inquest, I stood in front of a mirror dressed in a suit. Though I felt the heaviness of stress, I also felt oddly calm. Police officers soon arrived at our house to pick me up, and we drove to the large downtown courthouse. We pulled into a private parking area and I was ushered into a quiet waiting room on one of the top floors. I had several officers with me for support as I waited to testify.

The minutes seemed like an eternity as they ticked by. I watched as my scheduled time approached and then passed the hour mark. I knew it would be any minute. I felt my nerves and adrenaline flooding over me, and I briefly stepped into a restroom to pray. Moments later I saw the court deputy walk past the window to the door of our room. He opened the door and simply said "They're ready."

My full-time partner, who had been working the extra duty the day of the shooting, was with me. He patted my shoulder in support, and I followed the deputy down the hall to a private stairwell which led down to the courtroom. As we walked down the stairs, my knees suddenly felt weak, as if they were going to buckle. Anxiety filled me to the core of my being, and I wondered how I could even get through this. I prayed and asked God for strength. With amazing clarity, a specific passage from the Bible immediately came to my mind. It was the account of Jesus walking on water. During at account, the disciple Peter got out of the boat and started to walk on the water toward Jesus, but as he took his eyes off Jesus, looking instead at the wind and waves around him, he started to sink. Jesus quickly stretched out his hand and rescued Peter, but asked him, "Why did you doubt me?"

I realized that I was starting to sink, and God was reminding me to have faith that He was in control. My eyes were starting to focus on the "wind and waves" of the storm, and I needed to get my eyes back on Him. Almost instantly I felt strength returning to my legs as we finished the final steps toward the courtroom.

When we entered the main hallway, several members of the media stood outside the courtroom with cameras. I was ushered into the large courtroom, which was packed with people. I saw many faces of police officers and friends from the church and community, as well as a large number of angry faces. The inquest was televised, and cameras were spread throughout the room. I took the stand and looked out at the courtroom. I tried to focus on the faces of support, and not on those who were scowling at me with anger. As I started to testify, I was incredibly nervous, but eventually I felt an overwhelming sense of peace.

I really can't remember much of what was said when I was on the witness stand. Occasionally, when I see pictures, I can recall some details, but it is strangely hazy. I do remember leaving the courtroom and being incredibly grateful that it was over. As I left, my partner Cliff hugged me and told me how proud he was of me.

The next morning, Jennifer, Jack, and I headed to the airport. We were scheduled to get out of town to Montana to decompress. The inquest was a large hurdle behind us, and we finally entered a lull. As we waited at the airport, I saw my photo on the front page of all the newspapers in the newsstands. The last 24 hours had been a whirlwind, and I was wearing the same clothes as when I testified - not the greatest choice. "Oh great," I thought as we headed to our gate. While waiting to board the plane, we sat down in some open seats as far away as we could from anyone else. While we waited it seemed like every person was staring at us. We tried to ignore it, and Jack was a good distraction. As a baby, he was giggling and happy, and we focused our attention on him rather than on our audience. I couldn't help noticing that everyone was reading newspapers. Just about everywhere I looked, someone had a paper open with my picture front-and-center. I just wanted to leave for Montana and get away from everything.

We finally boarded the plane, and I rested my head back on the seat, my mind churning with a months-worth of trying events. I was exhausted. Jennifer was exhausted. I looked over at her and Jack and thanked God for them. By the end of the day, we had made our connecting flights and we landed in Billings. As we walked into the terminal and were greeted by family, I felt like I wanted to cry. Finally, we could decompress.

Talk At A Coffee Shop

The months after the shooting were stressful in a way I had never experienced before. After the inquest, the media coverage died down, which was a weight lifted from my mind. I was still on routine administrative leave while the numerous other levels of review were completed. The days and weeks were strangely sporadic and without routine. For my own health, I kept a fairly strict routine at home. Some days were full of meetings and phone calls, and others were radio silence. I never really got used to it. Sometimes it felt like an eternity while I waited to hear when I could come back to work, and which assignment options would be available for me.

During this time, our family didn't venture out much. We spent time working on things around the house, and I volunteered at our church. After having my picture on display with all of the negative attention, we were always slightly on edge when we went out and about. Several times, while at the grocery store or doing other businesses, strangers approached me and offered words of support and encouragement. Every time I saw someone approaching me, I felt my adrenaline flowing. I didn't want to be paranoid, but I knew I needed to be watchful and I couldn't be complacent. Jennifer and I prayed daily for God's protection on our family.

One day I was meeting a friend at a coffee shop close to our home. The shop was busy, and we stood and visited in the long line while we waited for our order. Out of the corner of my eye I caught a man rapidly walking toward me through the crowd. I immediately turned my body to face him. His jaw and fists were clenched, and he glared at me for a second. Then in a loud voice he bellowed, "You're a murderer. A stone-cold killer!"

I felt like I was in a movie scene with every other noise screeching to a halt. The man's voice boomed as he continued with more ugly and hateful comments. My face felt hot with embarrassment, and it seemed like everyone was staring at me. When he finished his tirade, I looked him directly in the eyes. I had so much that I wanted to say to him, but I realized there were very few things that would change his mind and bring peace to the situation. I simply replied, "I'm sorry you feel that way. I'll pray for you."

The man held my gaze for a moment longer, and he remained silent. He grabbed his coffee and angrily walked out of the shop. To this day, he is the only person that has ever approached me in public to express anger. I did pray for the man that day, and I actually have prayed for him many times since. Maybe someday we will cross paths again, and perhaps we can sit down over a cup of coffee in peace.

Served

As time went by, I experienced many ups and downs. Some days I felt that I could rest, and other days I felt on-edge, waiting for the next hammer to drop. I was on a rollercoaster of emotions, and I'm grateful for many the people who helped me to stay grounded so I could maintain a clear perspective. I often found it very difficult to detach myself from negative conversations. There were well-meaning cops who would call or stop by to vent about all the misinformation and false narratives surrounding the story. I appreciated their support, but I found that their conversations left me with a feeling of heaviness and discouragement. I know this wasn't their intent, and I can now see how that it was just their way of processing it all.

One afternoon, I heard a loud knock at my front door. I figured it was a neighbor or a cop stopping by for a visit. I quietly made my way to the door and looked through peephole. I could see it was a young man in a t-shirt, but I didn't recognize him. I decided to go out through my garage and see what he wanted. I startled him, and immediately saw that he had a hostile and disheveled look. I felt on-edge as I watched his hands and I watched for any indication that he might be armed.Without hesitation he approached me and asked, "Are you Jason Sery?" He projected an astounding level of arrogance for someone who I had never met, and I replied, "Who are you?"

The young man repeated, "Are you Jason Sery?" We had a few more words, and he tried to hand me a folder of papers. I kept my distance and told the man to leave my property. He twisted his face into a scowl, and he muttered a few more words as he set the papers on the ground and walked away.

When he was gone, I retrieved the papers and found out that I had been served papers for a multimillion-dollar civil suit. I stood in my garage and read through them. The burden felt heavy, and I prayed before I went inside to tell Jennifer about it. I recall standing in our kitchen discussing it, the sun shining on the counter through the window, while Jack was happily playing in the family room. It was a moment of clarity for me about what truly matters, and I felt God's peace.

CHAPTER 14:

REDEFINING ADVERSITY

B eing a police officer affects our entire identity. It can become all-consuming, and that's where it is dangerous place to camp. But it is almost unavoidable. The truth is that the job will certainly become a huge part of who we are. This is why it is imperative to remember that this career will someday come to an end for all of us. I hold firmly that greatest overall wellness and resiliency for cops is rooted in an identity greater than the job. This isn't a new view for me. I saw this early in my career. While I'm very grateful for this job, and I love it, I also recognize that it could change or end at any point. This isn't a point of fact to dwell on, but it is a reality that stays well-kept in my mind.

The shooting investigation took several months to complete. It went through several official levels of review, internally and externally. One day I received a phone call from the Chief of Police, and we discussed the plan for me to return to work. There were several options, and I found the phone call encouraging and energizing. I was eager to go back, and after the call Jennifer and I discussed the various options. We decided to talk with a few other people before a decision was made. By then, we were definitely feeling better than we had during the several previous months.Later that day I received another phone call. It was the lead pastor at our church. "Jason," he said, "Do you have time to meet up today? I want to run something by you."

His voice was positive and upbeat. Our church had been a rock of support to us during those the months, and he and I made plans to meet later that afternoon. When I arrived at the pastor's office, he invited me to sit outside on the lawn next to his office. He had set out a couple chairs in a shaded area, and it was a perfect summer day. We spent a few minutes casually catching up, and then his faced turned serious. He pulled a piece of paper out of a folder and handed it to me. The top of it read:

"Men wanted for hazardous journey. Low wages, bitter cold, long hours of complete darkness. Safe return doubtful. Honour and recognition in event of success."

My eyes scanned it further and I read the rest of it. I looked up at my pastor and his eyes were staring intently at me. "Jason, I want to offer you a job here at the church."

He went on to describe a variety of roles and opportunities to work with people, but specifically middle-school students to start. I was shocked. It was the last thing I thought we were meeting about, and I felt a wide range of emotions going through me. We talked for over an hour about the details of this opportunity, and it ended with him praying for me.

As I left, he said, "Take some time to think about it, pray about it, and talk it over with Jennifer."

The short drive home was a blur, and my thoughts bounced between the two conversations that day.

Going Away And Coming Back

I had never even considered leaving police work. Even with all the stress and pressures of the previous months, I still desired to stay in the profession. During the time away from active duty, I had volunteered at some of the summer youth and sports camps at the church, and I had really enjoyed it. It was truly a privilege to be a role model and example for the kids. Now I was being offered a job to do it full-time. Jennifer was just as shocked as I was to hear about the offer. We felt we had a lot to consider, so we decided to take another trip back to Montana.

For me, Montana remains a place to get away and to gain clarity. Nearly every day we were there, I hiked around the top of the rimrocks surrounding they city. I had so many memories there, all the way back to high school when my dad was transferred there from out of state. Looking across the city and the valley, I thought of all the twists and turns in my life. My mind was flooded with memories. From my vantage point, I could see my old high school, the USMC recruiting office where I had joined the Marines, the college Jennifer and I attended, the cemetery where we buried my mom, and the streets I had worked as a young police officer.

I remembered the moment I decided to apply at several large police agencies in different states, and was quickly hired in Portland, Oregon. Jennifer was born and raised in Montana, but at the time we both felt it was the right opportunity. Now here I was, considering another large decision. It weighed on me. By the end of our trip, I decided to take the job at the church. It was a result of my belief that my identity was larger than being a cop, but I was still nervous.

I was excited about this new chapter, but I also wondered how it would be perceived by others, especially my fellow cops. Would they think I was running? Would they be supportive? At the end of the day, I had to rest in the fact that I was supported by my close family and friends, and I needed to take the next steps.

Over the next few weeks, we put things in order. I resigned as a police officer and started my new job at the church. It was a huge step of faith for us as a family, especially as the new job came with a huge pay cut. Still, Jennifer and I both felt it was the right decision. After my resignation, the police association held a get-together with an awesome send off. I had the opportunity to connect with countless cops, and the association presented our family with a gift to help offset some expenses. It was humbling, and I was incredibly thankful. I drove home feeling a strange blend of excitement about this new opportunity, and a feeling of sadness as I recalled the faces of those I was leaving. My mind clicked through the memories working with this group of exceptional men and women, and I hoped I was making the "right" decision.

Within about a year of working in my new position at the church, I started missing police work. Occasionally people would ask if I thought I would ever go back to being a cop, and I would say definitely no. I believed I was in the place I was supposed to be, but a part of me wondered if my "no" really should be a "maybe." I regularly connected with cops, and I felt torn between missing the job and remaining content to work at the church. At the two-year mark away from police work, more and more opportunities began to open for me at the church. I got a bump in my pay, along with several more responsibilities. However, I couldn't shake my desire to go back to police work.

When I finally decided to tell Jennifer, I didn't know how she would react. She had been through a lot, and we now had two kids, with our daughter Sophie being born within a year after I had left policing. Her response was unexpectedly encouraging. She said she was all-in. She told me that she felt being a police officer was my calling, and even with all the struggles and challenges, it was where I should be. The level of support from her was energizing. Still, we had to really think this through. Was going back to being a cop really a viable option? Did I want to start over again? My civil suit was still pending, and though I had been indemnified and supported by the city and agency, it still felt like there were many loose ends. We made another trip to Montana.

Over the next several months, we talked, we prayed, and we considered several options. I decided to apply with a mid-sized agency in Oregon. This was the city where our home, church, and school were located. The Chief at the time was well-known. I had never met him, but I remembered that he had sent me a personal card of support and encouragement after the shooting. Much later on, after I was hired and was off my probationary period, I talked to him about his card. I thanked him for being bold with his support. In his confident way, he just smiled and shook my hand.

Being back to work as a cop felt so good. I had been away from the job for three years, and in some ways, it felt like a new job. But it also felt like I was back with an old friend.

My first night back on patrol was a throwback to my first shift 12 years earlier. I felt all the excitement of a new cop, along with my veteran street experience and savvy to keep my nerves at bay. We were nearly done with a busy shift and we were headed back to the station to complete our paperwork when I noticed a man riding a bicycle on a side street. He was riding with no lights, and I saw him commit several traffic violations. I confirmed with my FTO that he was good with us making the stop, and we stopped the man on the side of the road. Within a minute or so we discovered that he had warrants for his arrest. As we attempted to place him in handcuffs, he broke free, and the foot pursuit was on. With a team effort, he was apprehended a short distance away. Welcome back to police work.

Redefining Adversity

The entire process of this ordeal has helped me begin a journey into redefining adversity, struggles, and decision making. It's easy to let adversity beat us down, but we can truly find strength and perseverance through it. Having an awareness of how we are wired, knowing how we tend to react to adversity, and having support from others, are all keys to developing a life where adversity actually strengthens and helps to mold us instead of defeating us. When a mindset has been forged that is at peace with adversity and struggles as a part of life, we can be comfortable with being uncomfortable. But worries and anxieties are barriers to this kind of growth. I can easily fall into worrying about what struggle or "bad thing" is coming next, waiting for the next shoe to drop. Down the road, I usually find that my anxiety or worry was baseless and needless. That's not to say that we shouldn't anticipate difficulties, or reasonably prepare for them when we can, but worry and anxiety has many physical, emotional, and spiritual side-effects.

In Matthew 6:25-34 Jesus talks about the futility of worrying. In verse 27, He asks, "Can all your worries add a single moment to your life?" He ends verse 34 saying, "So don't worry about tomorrow, for tomorrow will bring its own worries. Today's trouble is enough for today." (NLT)

Simple, but not easy. I routinely find it necessary to take inventory of my thoughts and evaluate whether I'm falling into a pattern of worry versus faith and trust. There are so many things we can't control, and many of the things we think we can control are also ultimately out of our hands. This is a moment-by-moment process because life only comes to us one moment after the next, one breath at a time, once heartbeat followed by another. I've discovered that when I consciously evaluate what I'm anxious or worried about, and honestly assess if I can change things, I typically find I'm wasting time and energy on something that gives me no return. I'm still learning to let go of things outside my span of influence and control. It has helped me to redefine adversity.

Decision Making

This way of thinking has translated into many of my life decisions. We can wrestle with decisions for days on end, overthinking matters to death, and the result may be analysis paralysis. We get stuck in the mire of indecision. We need to weigh the effects of our decisions without getting weighed down by them. Creating a list of pros and cons, getting input from trusted people in our lives, and praying about it are healthy ways of making decisions. But sometimes I fall back into my old pattern of sorting through every "what if" scenario and painting it with the darkest of possibilities. This is a working definition of worry. But when I pause and ask myself simple questions from a logical and conscious perspective, the "what if's" are rarely troubling. I've learned that most of my battle comes from either one of three fears: change, the unknown, or failure.

These are the realities and risks that decision-making forces us to face. But when we embrace them with forward-thinking and faith, we usually find that great rewards are waiting for us around the next corner. Even if a decision we make turns out to be different than you'd hoped for, most courses can be corrected. It may take time, money, energy, and humility, but our worst-case scenarios are often not as extreme as we believe they are. Anticipating a change can be more challenging than the change itself.

Why We Do This

One day I was at a local gym playing my tunes and enjoying a good workout. As I glanced around the large fitness center, I noticed a man sitting on a piece of workout equipment looking in my direction. He appeared to be in his early 50's, and he had a face that looked weathered from a difficult life. He sported a sleeveless t-shirt which displayed several tattoos on his arms. He looked away when we made eye contact. I could tell he had been on the other side of the law, and I kept a peripheral eye on him as I did my next set of exercises. After completing the set, I saw the man get up and walk toward me. I turned to face him as he walked right up and smiled. "How's the crime fighting business?" he asked. My mental rolodex of people I've arrested spun out of control as I tried to place who this man was.

"Good." I replied.

The man extended his hand and said, "I just wanted to come over and thank you." He told me that I had arrested him over two years ago for crimes related to several addictions that he was battling. He recounted that the words I shared with him, and the dignity I showed him had helped change his life. He told me he had given his life over to God, and with the help of Him and counseling, he had broken free from the grips of addiction. In addition, he said that God had worked to reconcile him to his estranged wife and had provided him with much-needed employment. Tears began to fill his eyes as he shaped the details of our conversation from over two years earlier. I was stunned. I could only vaguely remember my conversation with this man.

Throughout my years as a cop, I've regularly talked on a personal level with people that I have arrested. I am always curious and intrigued by the decisions and path that they had taken, which ultimately brought us to connect. Most are sad stories, fraught with addiction, poor choices, and abuse. Some of the people are honest, some are liars, and all are broken. I usually end up sharing a few words of encouragement with them, and I tell them I will pray for them. It's my practice to quietly say a quick prayer after I leave them, knowing I may never see that person again. Most of the time have no idea if our conversation has had any effect on them.

On this particular day, I was reminded that those conversations do make a difference. In a world and in a profession that are inundated by cynicism, it's easy to get trapped in the negative cycle and lose all empathy. Without question, there is sheer evil in this world, and there will always be criminals who need to be locked away forever. But I've seen that many of the people we encounter are simply hurting and broken. That moment in the gym was a pointed reminder to me that each day counts, and our compassion for people has great affect, even if we don't see it. This is part of the process of redefining adversity.

CHAPTER 15:
COFFEE AND AMISH POPCORN

There is something uniquely awesome about simplicity. There is also something uncomfortable about it. When we live with simplicity, it's freeing and refreshing. So why do we avoid it and complicate our lives in a twisted belief that simplicity will somehow reduce us to a lesser life? I've found that simplicity is a necessity. It actually bolsters my life. A hectic, busy, complex life may work for a time or a season, but rarely does it bring me the life I really want. It doesn't deliver on its promises. It's the same kind of lie we believe about retirement. We think, if we can only get through this "season," then we will finally get to a perfect place in life. But we know that's not how life really works.

I'm not talking about laziness. I've known people who have fallen into the trap of thinking "the simple life" is a perpetual state of ease, and even unemployment. Always dreaming about the good life, they never move toward a goal. A hectic life saps energy away, and a lazy life dulls it to death.

It's good to regularly assess and adjust our lives according to our true needs. There are two Bible verses that have regularly spoken to me as I evaluate my goals and aspirations. They have helped me to recognize blind spots in myself and to gain a clear, simple perspective. Look at Psalm 46:10: "Be still and know that I am God! I will be honored by every nation. I will be honored throughout the world." Some versions translate the first part of the verse, "Cease striving." God has used this short verse to remind me that He is in control of everything in the universe, not to mention every aspect my life. But sometimes I think and act like I don't believe it. I still get worried and bothered by so many things. I so easily forget the simplicity of trusting Him.

The next passage is found in Proverbs 28:19: "A hard worker has plenty of food, but a person who chases fantasies ends up in poverty." Hard work is deeply satisfying. The road to plenty is to simply work hard. Chasing fantasies is like chasing after wind. In the end, there is nothing to grab onto, and having nothing will leave you feeling empty at the end of life. Then, in a flash, life is gone. I'm constantly assessing and adjusting my priorities to find the tipping point between these two verses.

Several years ago, our family was visiting my in-laws after they had moved to Ohio. Their home is near a large Amish community, and my father-in-law had developed friendships with a few Amish neighbors. He routinely hired them to help with different projects, and during our visit one of the Amish families invited us to their home. I later learned that this is very rare, as the Amish community is extremely closed and tight knit. However, my father-in-law had developed trust with this particular family, and they were excited to open their home to us. When we drove up the driveway to their farmhouse, I immediately noticed that it was very clean and well-kept. The family greeted us and invited us inside. We sat in their living room and visited with them. The kids lit oil lamps as evening set in and then made popcorn on the stove. As we sat and ate Amish popcorn, we talked about our families and our lives. The boys had a million questions about police work, and I shared exciting stories of catching bad guys and helping people. It was a memorable evening, and I feel blessed to have experienced it. A couple hours later we said our goodbyes, and we drove away down their long driveway. I looked in the rearview mirror and I could see the family outside watching us leave.

Though many things about the Amish life and customs remain strange to me, the word that struck me most about them was "simple." This family was full of incredibly hard workers, and yet they had a very simple life. There is freedom in simplicity.

The Need For Silence

The world is too noisy. It is probably noisier than ever before. At least, the level of noise seems to infiltrate our lives more these days. In our society, we have a constant stream of social media, news, and data flowing through our minds. My daughter and I were recently flying back home from Montana after a visit. Airports are fun places to people watch. When we were catching a connecting flight in a major airport, we sat and watched people in the busy terminal. The vast majority of the people – moving, sitting, and standing

– were glued to their phones. Several people nearly collided with others as they absentmindedly walked around with no spatial awareness.

As cops, we know about the uptick in traffic crashes since the development of smart phones. I love my smart phone, and it has made communication quick and easy for me. However, easiness isn't the same as simplicity. Watching people in a busy airport terminal nowadays just isn't what it used to be.

I enjoy recalling the technological advancements during my career. When I first started in the mid-90's, many agencies, including the one I worked for, didn't have computers in patrol cars. When an officer wanted to check a license plate or see if a person had warrants, it was all done via police radio through a dispatcher or through support personnel at the police department. Some officers became savvy masters at analyzing scars, tattoos, and other physical indicators to determine a person's identity from a teletype warrant. I know some great street cops who even became proficient at analyzing fingerprints. They developed the ability to examine a suspect's fingerprints on the street, and they could quickly confirm whether a person was lying about their identity. It's impressive to watch these masters at work. But it's one of many things in police work that advancements in technology have changed. With new technology, most agencies now have devices and computers that quickly bring up DMV photos, booking photos, or even social media photos, to determine a person's identity. The old street-smart techniques aren't used or needed much anymore. But some of the technological advancements now used in policing can become a crutch, and even a distraction. I've watched new officers getting so focused on the computer data, route maps, and other technology, that they miss things that are right in front of their noses. I believe the best Field Training Officers and training programs will find a blend between new technology and sticking with old-fashioned street smarts.

Technology and instant information have made a contribution to our professional proficiency and our personal wellness, but they can also lure us into unhealthy behaviors. As I mentioned earlier, after a long work shift, or after coming home from a day of trauma and tragedy, it's easy to just sit down and scroll through social media, watch YouTube videos, or to chill and click the remote. Not bad things in themselves, but not always good at certain times or after certain days. We can find ourselves using technology to decompress and cope with the hard things we've experienced, and the information we take into our brains through these sources is often negative and toxic.

I've been there many times. So, at the end of a day, I make a conscious effort to not indulge in social media, news, and things that can spin me up. Instead, I find it's important to be intentional about doing other things. Getting a workout in, reading, spending time in lighter conversation with family and friends, can all be refreshing and helpful when we need to decompress.

As cops, this is nothing we haven't heard before. It's just a reminder. We need lots of reminders.

We also need silence. We are bombarded with the "noise" day-in and day-out. We need pure, simple silence. It's essential to our well-being, like a glass of clean, cold water. But we also need to learn how to live with silence. We've become so accustomed to listening to the noise, it seems counterintuitive and even stressful to listen to nothing but silence. So, I've had to become intentional about being alone with my quiet thoughts, without technology or distractions. I'm finding it refreshing.

When I first started sitting still in silence, I discovered that my mind was a chatterbox, constantly shouting about all the tasks that needed doing. My mind raced from one thought to the next. But gradually I developed a habit of enjoying my times of silence. They have become a coveted part of my day, and I protect these times dearly. I have my times of silence in the early morning hours, before anyone else is up. Some of these times are longer than others. I don't have an exact routine to follow. This is when I pray, read, think, and simply consider the blessings in my life. It's become such a great part of my day, I will even turn down opportunities for an early morning coffee, or other invitations, just so I can keep my alone time.

Not everybody's schedule would allow for an early morning quiet time, and no two people are wired alike, so you'll need to figure out what works best for yourself. But you may have already figured out that you need a time of silence. That's the first step. You may also need to ease into it, taking just a few minutes during your day. It's strange to say, but seeking silence is not a natural act. But it may be something you've been wanting without even realizing it. And it's the small, private steps we take that can lead us to long-term health, wellness, and resiliency in this career.

Hobbies Beyond The Job

One of my closest friends, a veteran officer, recounted to me a conversation he had with a well-known police psychologist in our area. He said the psychologist stated that, when she asks cops about their hobbies and activities outside the job, many of them struggle to come up with anything of substance. Cops will often say, "I work out," or, "I like to spend time outdoors," or "I spend time with my family." But nailing down how often they do these activities, and whether or not it is a job-related activity or a true hobby, can be a different story.

Some literature on police wellness describes how cops gradually move away from activities and hobbies they had once enjoyed prior to entering their profession. It's usually a slow process where these things just slowly and imperceptibly fade away from their everyday lives. It's like that misguided ship that moves off course by just a fraction of one degree, and then loses its bearings.

I've learned that I need to have real hobbies as much as I need my times of silence. This means that I need to intentionally make time for enjoyable activities outside of my job. In my busy life, it also means that I need to schedule it and make it non-negotiable. Unfortunately, our good intentions and best-laid plans can be interrupted by a call for an over-time shift or some other work-related issue. We need to establish personal boundaries to protect ourselves from ourselves.

I enjoy working in my yard, and I don't mean yard work. I enjoy designing and landscaping my yard, especially ponds. Jennifer might have a different outlook on some of the ponds I've built, but it's a great hobby and a welcome escape for me. Hobbies may sound like a form of torture to some, but it's incredibly healthy to find another side of yourself in a hobby or a fun activity. You might even discover how enjoyable it can be to get lost in something that lets you simply be yourself again.

Finding Joy Daily

Chaplain Jim McGuire has been my mentor for many years. God has used his wisdom and influence to keep me on course and to help me get a clear perspective in a variety of situations. Jim and I met decades ago, when I was a teenager. For a few years, my dad was stationed in Oregon, and our family bounced around checking out local churches. My parents finally settled on one close to our home. The church had a vibrant middle and high school youth program, and Jim was the pastor who was overseeing them. The church held an event called Raft Rally each summer, and one year I was able to attend with some friends. Raft Rally was a week-long event with rafting, sports, hiking, and hearing good speakers talking about interesting topics. It was life-changing for me. For the first time in my life, my faith became my own during that week. That's when I gave my life to Jesus Christ.

I had grown up in a Christian home, and I knew how to say the right things and how to act in conformity to my parents' beliefs. But as I entered my teen years, I had a nagging feeling that I should personally look into matters of faith. During the Raft Rally, one of the speakers, a pro-football player, told how he once had this same "feeling." This took me by surprise, and so I started looking more seriously into the Christian faith for myself. The closer I looked at Jesus Christ, the more deeply personal my faith became. God showed me what true forgiveness is through His Son. One night while I lay awake in my tent, I prayed and asked God to forgive me for the things I had done wrong. I asked Him to change me into the person I was meant to be. From that point on, I knew that I was a different person inside myself. But I I also knew I would still struggle living out my faith.

A fallacy presented by some about the Christian faith is that it is a "cure-all." They say that all your troubles will be wiped away, you will have perfect peace, and God will provide everything you need. There is truth to this message, but there's more to it than that. The full truth is that life is messy. We all have troubles, sometimes around every corner.

When people ask if I'm religious, I tell them no, I'm a man of faith. To me, there is a big difference. Religion revolves around rules and rituals and lists of "do's and don'ts." It may be well-intended, but the motivation behind "getting right with God" is fear and guilt. This inevitably leads into a vicious cycle of failure, defeat and discouragement. But simple faith is different. My faith and hope are anchored in God's commitment to me through his Son. My standing with Him doesn't depend on my commitment to Him, but rather, it depends on His commitment to me. This is why I have peace with God. It isn't achieved by keeping rules, nor by how I feel about myself or my circumstances. It's recognizing that I truly don't have anything to offer God in order to be right with Him. Some things in life are too precious to be bought, earned or begged for. God's free gift of grace and forgiveness in Jesus Christ is priceless. It is what I desperately want and need every day.

I can't improve on how the Bible puts it: "And let us run with endurance the race God has set before us. We do this by keeping our eyes on Jesus, the author and perfecter of our faith." (Hebrews 12:1-2)

Many years after that Raft Rally, Jim retired from the church and took a position at our department as a police chaplain. On one of his first ride-alongs, he jumped in the police car with me. It was surreal to see how God had reconnected us after many years. Jim is one of few police chaplains who can deeply connect with cops, community members, and people from all walks of life. He distinctly lives out his faith without pushing his beliefs on those he works with. To this day, Jim routinely helps me see life through a different lens. I tend to let my emotions drive my thinking. Feelings are a gift from our Creator. They are good, but they are not intended to be our sole guide in life, simply because they can go up and down like a rollercoaster. Jim has an amazing gift for helping me sort through my feelings and to bring things into proper perspective. I've met often met with him and discussed the challenges I'm facing. Jim listens and acknowledges whatever I may be going through. Then he brings me back around with a simple saying, "Don't let these things rob you of your joy."

I know first-hand that the challenges of life can be powerfully draining. Many times, the storms have seemed endless and insurmountable. But when they become my focus, they can rob me of the joy of each new day. Yes, joy can be found every day, even in the darkest and most hopeless days. It is found in God's unwavering and unshakeable promises, and Jim is always pointing me back to them. God has powerfully used him in my life, and I wouldn't be here today without him.

The Job Now

I'll say it again, cops are unique. The cops I know are smart, witty, and people savvy. I am continually amazed at how masterfully they can communicate and quickly transition during rapidly evolving situations. They drive forward day after day under extreme pressures. Police officers around our great nation are now under scrutiny and pressures like never before. A narrative that all police officers are evil and racist persists in the main-stream media. It's disheartening, and it takes a heavy toll on the men and women of this profession. Recently, two officers in California were ambushed and shot while sitting in their patrol car. The officers were in rushed into surgery at the hospital, with their children, families, and loved ones praying for their recovery and healing. During this time a hostile group met outside the hospital, and some in the crowd were heard shouting "I hope they f@#$% die," and, "Tell their family I hope they f!@#$% die."

This is a window into the era that we are working through as a profession. I know that the majority of people still support us, but I have never seen this level of widespread anger and hatred toward police. It saddens me. I know the hearts of those I serve with every day, and it's not the terrible narrative that is being portrayed. Yet, even with this difficult season upon us, officers are going out every day to protect and serve the people in their communities. But the added pressure of hatred and malice against them takes an enormous toll on a cop. Officers are experiencing a sense of personal hopelessness at crisis levels never seen before. I pray every day for our communities, and the men and women who tirelessly serve them.

A Good Path And Good News

"We are on a good path." The guys on my team have heard me say this numerous times. So often, in fact, they jokingly say it with me. Sometimes I've said it just to verbalize my positivity, but it's also what I truly believe. Even a good path can have bumps, potholes, and dangers seen and unseen. This is the reality of life, and many obstacles are draped in camouflage. Left to our own navigation, the path of this life is unclear, deceptive, and full of wrong turns, which often bring confusion and despair. I believe the good path is one that is lit up and directed by the One who loves and cares for us just as we are.

Two scripture verses that have helped me to keep trusting and thinking forward are: "Your word is a lamp to my feet and a light to my path." (Psalm 119:105) And also, "The mind of man plans his way, but the Lord directs his steps." (Proverbs 16:9)

I can't stress it enough: we have to be bigger than ourselves. We can't walk alone. To the core of my being, I believe it's essential to have others walk with us on this journey. Without God's help and grace, I don't believe it's possible to navigate our way and finish strong. My hope is that the words and experiences between these pages will bring encouragement, perspective, and strength to those who have walked the journey as peace officers. This is a truly great and noble profession. I'll close with a letter.

To My Cop Brothers And Sisters:

You are my heroes. Thank you for the work you do day-in and day-out. Thank you for staying the course, and doing what is often a thankless job, despite extreme adversity, media scrutiny, and tense, uncertain, and rapidly evolving situations. Thank you for hearing your calling. To those who have walked this path before us, thank you. Thank you for holding the line. Thank you for living and keeping to the core values of courage, compassion, and integrity. You have made a difference. Your example and walk have provided inspiration, and it helps give us strength to stay the course.

To those of us who are now walking this path, continue to hold the line. The storm and the noise are raging around us – seemingly more than ever before – but now is the time to stand firm. We know there will always be the few who tarnish the badge and the oath we have sworn to uphold. Remember the truth – those are not the majority! Keep perspective, serve others with grace, strength, and honor. Continue to give light to the path for those who are just starting out and coming after us.

To those preparing to start this journey to walk this great path, don't forget that this is a high calling with great responsibility. Remember why you signed up for this job. Remember the details of the oath you took. Stay humble. Keep integrity as a cornerstone of your character, and never lose your love for people. Strive to walk in their shoes. Bring with you a perfect blend of compassion and justice.

To each of us – live bigger than yourself. Commit to serving others for your entire life. By God's grace, keep your character and integrity as prized possessions. And when the darkness sets in, know you are not alone. Know that this is the time to link your armor with those in this journey with you. May you overcome the fear and lies that try to prevent you from reaching out. Stay humble. Find strength through adversity. Don't let circumstances rob you of your joy, and may God's amazing grace shine upon you all your days.

❖ Jason Sery - Christian, Husband, Father, Cop...and More.

ACKNOWLEDGEMENTS

To my editor Jim Morud:

You are one of the most accomplished and humble men I know. Your stories of world travels and sharing your faith in Christ are inspirational and life-changing. Thank you for your keen eye, wisdom, and encouragement.

To my extended family and friends:

I am tremendously blessed to have all of you in my life. Your prayers and friendships have helped me through the darkness. Thank you for your on-going love and support.

To my brothers and sisters with boots on the ground:

Thank you for what you do every hour of every day. Your dedication, talents, and abilities are amazing, and I'm humbled to serve with you. I pray God continues to protect and bless the peacemakers.

To Jim McGuire:

I am still in awe of how God re-connected us after so many years and so many life events. You are an inspiration, and I would not be where I am without you. Thank you for your unwavering example of faithfulness, strength, and discernment.

To Brick:

You are a brother at all times. Thank you for being there in my darkest hours.

Made in the USA
Coppell, TX
05 June 2021

56931579R00098